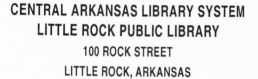

Consult Them in the Matter

Consult Them in the Matter

A NINETEENTH-CENTURY ISLAMIC ARGUMENT
FOR CONSTITUTIONAL GOVERNMENT

The *Muqaddima* (Introduction) to *Ithaf Ahl al-Zaman
bi Akhbar Muluk Tunis wa ʿAhd al-Aman*
(Presenting Contemporaries the History of the
Rulers of Tunis and the Fundamental Pact)
by Ahmad ibn Abi Diyaf

Translated from the Arabic
with Introduction and Notes
by L. Carl Brown

The University of Arkansas Press
Fayetteville
2005

09   08   07   06   05   5   4   3   2   1

Text design by Ellen Beeler

⊗ The paper used in this publication meets the minimum requirements of the
American National Standard for Permanence of Paper for Printed Library
Materials Z39.48-1984.

Library of Congress Cataloging-in-Publication Data

Ibn Abi al-Diyaf, Ahmad, 1804?–1874.
   [Ithaf ahl al-zaman bi akhbar muluk Tunis wa 'ahd al-aman. English.
   Selections]
   A nineteenth century Islamic argument for constitutional government : the
   muqaddima (introduction) to Ithaf ahl al-zaman bi akhbar muluk Tunis wa
   'ahd al-aman (Presenting contemporaries the history of the rulers of Tunis
   and the fundamental pact) / by Ahmad ibn Abi Diyaf ; translated from the
   Arabic with introduction and notes by L. Carl Brown.
       p. cm.
   Includes bibliographical references.
   ISBN 1-55728-803-8 (alk. paper)
   1. Tunisia—History—1516–1881. 2. Ahmad, Bey of Tunis, 1861 or 2–1942
   or 3. I. Brown, L. Carl (Leon Carl), 1928– II. Title.
   DT263.I263132 2005
   961.1—dc22
                                                                    2005015337

"If you had been rough and hard-hearted they would have dispersed away from you. So forgive them and ask them to forgive you and consult them in the matter."

— *Qur'an 3:159*

Acknowledgments

I thank my Princeton University colleagues—Hossein Modarressi, Andras Hamori and Şukru Hanioglu— whose expertise helped me resolve many problems of translation, identification, and interpretation. It is also a pleasure to recall the work done on the text of the Fundamental Pact (*Ahd al-Aman*) many years ago by Elisabeth Robertson Kennedy (class of 1995). I am solely responsible for any remaining errors or infelicities.

L. Carl Brown
Princeton University

Contents

———◆———

Muqaddima to *Ithaf Ahl al-Zaman bi Akhbar Muluk Tunis wa ʿAhd al-Aman* by Ahmad ibn Abi Diyaf

———◆———

The numbers in parentheses in the text, from (1) to (77),
indicate the page in the published Arabic edition.

Translator's Introduction

Throughout the seventh decade of the nineteenth century, a Tunisian dedicated himself to writing a history of his country. The work began with a *Muqaddima* (Introduction), which was in fact a treatise on politics, addressing such questions as: Why is government necessary? What are the different forms of government? What is the best government? The author was no closet historian or political philosopher. He looked back on a half-century of governmental service to the beylik of Tunis. Not only did he write as an insider, he was a committed insider, being one of the principal figures in a small group of westernizing reformers.

The Tunisian who wrote this history was Ahmad ibn Abi Diyaf (known as Bin Diyaf). His history is entitled *Ithaf Ahl al-Zaman bi Akhbar Muluk Tunis wa ʿAhd al-Aman* (Presenting Contemporaries the History of the Rulers of Tunis and the Fundamental Pact) (Hereafter, *Ithaf*). Tunisia, at that time, was de jure a province in the Ottoman Empire but de facto an all but independent state with its own hereditary ruling family, bureaucracy, and military. Tunisia shared the plight common to the whole Ottoman Empire. It faced a neighboring Europe that was then, unlike in past centuries, capable of overwhelming the Muslim Mediterranean and was seemingly prepared to so act. The question "what is to be done?" posed by Bin Diyaf had relevance not just for those ruling in Tunis but also in Istanbul and Cairo, for Egypt was another de jure Ottoman provincial government that was independent de facto.

The *Ithaf* is a history with a thesis. Bin Diyaf seeks to show that the despotic rule of Muslim monarchs is the principal cause of the parlous condition of Tunisia, and that thesis is most clearly stated in the *Muqaddima* with which he begins his history.

Bin Diyaf was ideally situated to write this history. Born in Tunis in 1217 A.H. (1802–3), he was the only son of al-Hajj bil-Diyaf, a scribe *(katib)* in the Husaynid governmental bureaucracy. This meant that Bin Diyaf was born into a family in contact not only with government officials but also with the body of religious teachers and scholars who made up the ʿulama'. His father saw to it that he had the best education available in Tunis, and Bin Diyaf was clearly destined for either a career in religious scholarship or the scribal bureaucracy. When in 1827 Husayn Bey offered Bin Diyaf a position as governmental scribe, he readily accepted. Interestingly, his father protested the appointment, arguing that his son was still too young and inexperienced. Did the father want to see his son numbered among the ʿulama', which he may have seen as a safer position? Quite possibly, because the father had himself been ousted from office and imprisoned for a time in 1815 when his patron, the powerful Yusuf Sahib al-Tabiʿ, fell afoul of the bey and was summarily executed. Bin Diyaf, however, accepted the position and rose rapidly in the bureaucracy, soon becoming Husayn Bey's private secretary (*katib al-sirr*).

Having entered Tunisian government in 1827, remaining there until the 1870s and recording the history in his *Ithaf* to the year 1872, Bin Diyaf experienced at first hand the political history about which he wrote. He had lived through the ups and downs of Tunisia's wrestling with the challenges coming from Europe. His was not just an insider's view of those developments; he was a leading participant in the history he recorded.

Although Bin Diyaf never attained the top civil position of Chief Scribe (*bash katib*) he remained within the tight inner circle of government from the 1820s until 1864. His political history was enriched by an insider's perspective on the events he chronicled. Considering the time he spent within the small inner circle that made up Tunisian government, it is as if a Harry Hopkins, Arthur Schlesinger Jr., or Henry Kissinger had served not just a Roosevelt, Kennedy, or Nixon but all three presidents for an unbroken forty-year stint.

His last years replicated in milder form the difficulties faced by his father a half century earlier. He avoided the prison term suffered by his father, but after 1864 he was largely shunted aside, having lost favor with the reigning Muhammad al-Sadiq Bey, continuing his work with little responsibility and few duties until his retirement in 1872. He died two years later in October 1874.

BIN DIYAF, KHAYR AL-DIN AND IBN KHALDUN

Those years of the 1860s proved a blessing for Bin Diyaf the historian, for it was in just this period of being ousted from the inner circle of

Tunisian government that he found the time to begin the decade-long work of producing his history. Here the comparison with his great Tunisian predecessor, Ibn Khaldun (1332–1406), may be noted. Almost exactly a half millennium earlier Ibn Khaldun had found the necessary leisure to write his great philosophy of history when in exile after losing out in the always dangerous game of court politics.

Nor is this a whimsical comparison. Bin Diyaf was clearly inspired by Ibn Khaldun, who is cited more than any other source in his *Muqaddima*. Indeed, what would seem to be a conscious effort in nineteenth-century Tunisia to call up the spirit of Ibn Khaldun is revealed as well in yet another Tunisian political treatise published while Bin Diyaf was completing his *Ithaf*. This was *The Surest Path*[1] written by Khayr al-Din al-Tunisi, who led that small circle of Tunisian would-be westernizers to which Bin Diyaf belonged.

In all three cases the author had been an "insider" heavily involved in the politics of the day. All three at a later stage were obliged, or felt obliged, to abandon the corridors of power and thus found the time to write. All three wrote a *Muqaddima,* that of Ibn Khaldun being an essay in political philosophy or even, as has been suggested in modern times, a great work of political sociology. The *Muqaddimas* of Khayr al-Din and Bin Diyaf might properly be labeled political treatises.

There is, of course, an enormous difference of scale in the three *Muqaddimas.* Ibn Khaldun's *Muqaddima* fills three fat volumes in Arabic and in Franz Rosenthal's English translation.[2] Bin Diyaf's *Muqaddima* is really only a tract of seventy-seven pages in Arabic. Khayr al-Din's is eighty-nine pages in Arabic, just over one hundred in English translation. All three "Introductions" were followed by more conventional histories or, in the case of *The Surest Path,* what might be dubbed a comparative government text.

These three "Introductions" written by three "Tunisians" (in Ibn Khaldun's time what is now Tunisia was *Ifriqiyya,* the Arabization of the Roman term "Africa") all draw deeply on their author's knowledge of Tunisia and are, thus, useful for what they tell us about Tunisia. All three also evoke themes important to the understanding not just of Tunisian history but the history of the larger Middle East and North Africa. This claim needs to be briefly explained.

THE LARGER POLITICAL CONTEXT

The master narrative that most usefully organizes the political history of the Middle East and North Africa from the late eighteenth century until the First World War depicts a once-powerful imperial polity, the Ottoman Empire, finding itself no longer a match for its old neighbor and enemy—Europe. The Empire thus undertook a sustained endeavor, continuing over more than a century, to strengthen the state by adapting selected institutions and ideas of threatening Europe even while fighting wars and engaging in diplomacy in order to counter European intrusions. Yet, in a process that seems inexorable in retrospect, the Ottoman Empire was stripped of one province after another until soon after the First World War the last remaining Arab territories were surrendered to European control and the Anatolian core of the Ottoman Empire became the Republic of Turkey.

The history of the Middle East and North Africa, thus presented, concentrates on a very small number of individuals—the ruling elite—for it was those manning existing governments who were positioned first and most persistently to both perceive and respond to the challenges Europe presented. And they were governments, not a single government, for the sprawling Ottoman Empire contained two autonomous regimes—Egypt and Tunisia. Both were juridically Ottoman provinces, but their rulers exercised de facto autonomy if not independence, having their own militaries and their own governmental institutions.

These three different ruling elites based in Istanbul, Cairo, and Tunis varied greatly in size and strength. The rulers in Istanbul, however much weakened and dismembered by intrusive Europe, remained throughout the century in charge of a multinational empire, with holdings in the Balkans, Anatolia, and Arab lands.

Egypt under the Muhammad ʿAli dynasty aspired to empire, conquering Sudan to the south and even wresting Syria from its Ottoman suzerain in the 1830s, but thereafter stumbled, being forced from Syria in 1840 by European intervention. Later, Muhammad ʿAli's successors lost Sudan to the Mahdist revolt in the 1880s. Even before the Mahdist revolt, Egypt had fallen prey to outright European imperial rule in the form of a British "occupation" beginning in 1882 (formalized as a protectorate only in 1914 with the outbreak of the First World War).

Smallest of all, and surrounded by stronger neighbors, the beylik of Tunis sought to guard its precarious autonomy, which it lost in 1881 (just one year before Egypt), with the establishment of the French Protectorate.

For all their differences in size and situation, these three groups of ruling elites shared a common Ottoman political culture that by the nineteenth century had deep roots. Egypt had been incorporated into the Ottoman Empire as long ago as 1517 and Tunisia followed in 1574. These ruling elites were not only responding to a common threat coming from Europe, they were also drawing on a shared experience and worldview in facing that threat.

In all three cases, the responses and results of this confrontation with Europe followed a strikingly similar trajectory.[3] Governing elites in all three seized upon the idea of adapting European military methods as the answer to their weakened status vis-a-vis the old neighbor and enemy across the Mediterranean. Efforts at military modernization, in turn, provoked resistance from the traditional military, which had to be either destroyed or tamed. Thus, we find Muhammad ʿAli's massacre of Egypt's mamluks in 1811, Ottoman Sultan Mahmud's destruction of the Janissaries in 1826, and the less dramatic Tunisian integration of its Turkish and mamluk military class into European-style forces beginning in the 1830s.

To train the officers and soldiers for a European-style military force required such innovations as student missions to Europe and Western military training missions to the Middle East. Egypt and the Ottoman Empire chose both, while Tunisia relied on the latter. In all three cases this also entailed the creation of a small body of officials conversant in a European language (usually French) and the translation of European works.

By adopting the post–French Revolution notion of large armies raised by conscription of citizens, these ruling elites also moved away from the centuries-old concept of small professional forces manned by those ethnically, socially, and often even linguistically separated from the great mass of the subjects.

Conscription into larger armies, efforts to achieve military self-sufficiency by creating indigenous armament industries, and taking other steps to increase the size, scope, and expense of government created budgetary deficits. These were covered increasingly by loans from European banks, all on usurious terms. These loans that began in the 1850s were not amortized by economic growth, for the Middle Eastern economies in these years were as vulnerable to Europe's increasing economic and commercial clout as to Europe's military superiority. During these "take-off" years of Europe's industrial revolution, Europe's factories undercut in price and often quality what Middle Eastern artisans could produce. At the same time, the Middle East lacked anything equivalent to Europe's institutionalized credit facilities that might nurture capital formation and economic growth.

As a result, all three of these Middle Eastern regimes lapsed into state bankruptcy. Tunisia came first in 1869, Egypt and the Ottomans in the following decade. And in response to all three state bankruptcies the European state system moved in to impose debt collection commissions with intrusive European monitoring of the revenue and budgetary activities of the three affected states. This major surrender of state autonomy was soon to be followed by outright European colonial rule in Tunisia (1881) and Egypt (1882).

Only the central Ottoman Empire survived until just after the First World War. Even the Ottomans gained those extra four decades of precarious independence largely by the offsetting rivalries of the European states (the complex multilateral pattern of diplomacy that historians label "the Eastern Question").

In the narrow terms characterizing old-fashioned, Eurocentric diplomatic history (which gives us the old saw about the Ottoman Empire as the "sick man of Europe") this master narrative of the nineteenth–century Middle East offers a stark story. Three "states" with a shared political culture confronted a similar foreign challenge over an extended time period—well over a century for the central Ottoman state ruling from Istanbul, roughly three-quarters of a century for Egypt and Tunisia. All three efforts ended in defeat marked in two cases by the advent of direct European colonial rule. The third, the central core and the largest, which was the Ottoman Empire ruling from Istanbul, even ceased to exist. That final coup de grâce dispatching this remnant empire, which in territorial extent, duration, and cultural impact ranks with the Roman, Byzantine, and Abbasid Empires, was delivered by an Ottoman general, Mustafa

Kemal (Ataturk), who rallied the people of Anatolia to create instead a nation-state, the Republic of Turkey.

During this entire period, even while the issues of military modernization, wars and rumors of war, and state loans leading to bankruptcy dominated the thoughts and actions of the political elites ruling in Cairo, Istanbul, and Tunis, another process was underway. Looking across the waters at Europe, these Middle Eastern political elites saw governments that were stronger, more efficient, and more popular. Was it because these governments were less arbitrary, ruled by law, and had means of involving others in advice and consent? Were such arrangements in any way against the tenets of Islam? The thoughts and actions moving in the direction of what can properly be dubbed constitutionalism emerged in this very context. Bin Diyaf's *Ithaf* fits into this overarching historical framework of three different "governments" of varying size and scope wrestling with similar challenges, coming up with similar responses and experiencing similar results. His history offers a perceptive insider's account of these developments as seen from Tunis, and his short *Muqaddima* is a disquisition on the forms and varieties of government that suggests what needs to be done to secure a more just and effective Tunisian (and, for that matter, Ottoman) government.

The Tunisia of which Bin Diyaf wrote can thus be seen as offering a case study relevant to similar political developments throughout the Ottoman Empire. Somewhat more detail on the specific Tunisia case is in order.

THE TUNISIAN CASE

Tunisia during these years offered a striking chronological correlation with Egyptian developments. The great westernizing effort in Tunisia, largely contemporaneous with that of Egypt's Muhammad ʿAli, took place during the reign of Ahmad Bey (1837–55). He was followed by a ruler who, just like ʿAbbas I in Egypt, sought to turn back the clock—Muhammad Bey (1855–59). Then came the Tunisian equivalent of Egypt's Saʿid, Muhammad al-Sadiq (1859–82). Rulers in both Egypt and Tunisia contracted European loans at roughly the same time, and the result for both was state bankruptcy, for Tunisia in 1869 and Egypt in

1876. Even the period during which the two regimes fell prey to outright European colonial rule is remarkably close, with Tunisia falling in 1881 and Egypt in 1882.

There are, even so, interestingly different twists to the Tunisian history. Ahmad Bey's ambitious military modernization effort achieved little, and also—unlike Egypt—Tunisia never advanced an adventurous foreign policy. To maintain a tenuous autonomy against the press of outside powers as well as the Ottomans (who in 1835 reestablished direct administration of neighboring Tripolitania) was challenge enough. And the intervention of European investors and adventurers, while influential, fell far short of the "Klondike" rush experienced on the banks of the Nile.[4]

Moreover, developments in the direction of parliamentary government followed a different trajectory. Tunisia actually had a brief period of would-be constitutional rule that was suspended in the wake of a wide-spread revolt throughout the countryside that almost toppled the Husaynid dynasty. Only after this did the most impressive, if brief, effort in governmental reform take place. This was the ministry of Khayr al-Din from 1873 to 1877. Thereafter, a short period of reactionary beylical autocracy ended when the French invaded Tunisia from neighboring Algeria and imposed a Protectorate in 1881.

The advent of this period ushering in a written constitution (the first in the modern Arab world, indeed in the Middle East) can be precisely dated—1857. In June of that year, Muhammad Bey's efforts to abandon the westernization pushed by his predecessor and revert to old-style beylical autocracy were abruptly halted by a decisive European intervention. A Jewish carter, one Samuel Sfez, making his way through the narrow streets of Tunis, ran over a Muslim child, and in the ensuing melee he allegedly blasphemed Islam. The bey insisted that the court invoke the harshest sentence—death—and Sfez was executed within a day. The bey's advisers had argued for a more lenient sentence, suggesting a possible European reaction, but the bey was adamant. Among other reasons for the bey's stance was that he had only recently approved the execution of a Tunisian soldier for having murdered a Jew.

Just as the bey's advisers had feared, the European reaction came immediately. For once the consular community spoke with one voice, this being one of the rare times when the usual rivalry between the British and

French consuls was put aside. A French naval vessel made a call at Tunis, and there were rumblings that the Ottomans planned to send ships as well. The bey, obliged to ensure that no such outrage could ever happen again, agreed to proclaim the ʿAhd al-Aman (translated into French as the *Pacte fondamentale*, a literal translation would be "Pledge of Security"). This document was patterned on the 1839 Ottoman *Hatt-ı Şerif* of *Gulhane*, the text of which Bin Diyaf included in his *Muqaddima*.[5]

The bey was also obliged to do more. He set up a working group to prepare a *qanun*, a constitution, to provide the rules for a consultative monarchy. The small group of Tunisian westernizing reformers, including Bin Diyaf, took the lead. The working group was to have six government officials and four ʿulamaʾ, but after the first meeting the ʿulamaʾ begged off. Such "political" activities, they maintained, were the responsibility of the bey and his entourage, not the ʿulamaʾ.[6] By the time the group drafting the constitution had completed its work, Muhammad Bey had died and been replaced by his brother, Muhammad al-Sadiq. Learning that Emperor Louis Napoleon III would be visiting Algeria, Muhammad al-Sadiq, on the advice of the French consul Leon Roche, arranged to meet the emperor in Algiers in September 1860, taking with him the draft constitution. Louis Napoleon graciously approved the constitution and medals were exchanged between the two and their entourages. The foreign dimension of Tunisian constitution-making could hardly be more evident: The ruler of one country traveled to meet the ruler of another and obtain his approval of the fundamental law to be adopted.

The constitution, proclaimed in April 1861, provided for a legislative body, the Grand Council, which could propose legislation that—if accepted by the ruler meeting with his council of ministers—would become law (Article 62). This would seem to offer merely an advisory role to the Grand Council, but Article 63 cites a wide-ranging number of actions (including promulgating new laws, raising or lowering taxes, abrogating existing laws, increasing the armed forces, changing the interpretation of a law, or dismissing an official) that could be taken only after having been submitted to the Grand Council for its consideration and approval. The ruler was specifically granted the right to appoint and dismiss officials as he chose (Article 14), and there was no explicit mention that such officials would be responsible to the Grand Council.

The Grand Council was singled out as the "guardian" of the ʿAhd al-Aman and the constitution. As for the ruler, should he violate the constitution then the allegiance pledged to him (al-bayʿa) was voided. These two stipulations, taken together, provided—ever so tentatively—the legislative body the right to call the ruler to account. At the same time, that body was unlikely to do so. All members were chosen by the government, and one-third were themselves government officials. Still, all in all, the principles of representation, consultation, and the rule of law that even the ruler must accept were in place. The very tame nature of the political participation just might have been an effective point of departure toward elective representation, limited perhaps at first to those of property, education or other such restrictions and only slowly moving toward universal suffrage. This could have been somewhat like the British experience from the time of the great Reform Bill of 1832 on into the twentieth century.

Such was not the fate of this constitution, which began its short life in a time of great economic hardship throughout the country. Only a handful of reformers within the bureaucracy and in Tunis, such as Khayr al-Din and Bin Diyaf, supported these changes. In the countryside, the ancien régime power structure of tribal shaykhs, village elders, and provincial governors saw the constitutional regime as impinging on their prerogatives. Most of all, the populace associated this new constitution with the increasingly harsh tax burden being levied. A principal revenue source, the *majba* tax had actually been doubled soon after the constitution was promulgated. In 1864 a revolt broke out in the countryside that almost overwhelmed the Husaynid dynasty. Muhammad al-Sadiq Bey survived, but the constitution did not.

Then, in 1873, by which time the beylik had been in virtual receivership following state bankruptcy in 1869, the leader of the westernizing reformers, Khayr al-Din, was given the opportunity to form a government. He held onto power until 1877, when a cabal of beylical courtiers and foreign interests obtained his dismissal. In those few years Khayr al-Din implemented an impressive number of reforms, especially in rationalizing the tax system (and stopping the annual military tax-collecting expeditions—the *mahalla*) and controlling abuses by government officials. He also took a number of seemingly small acts that actually had a huge and lasting effect. These included reorganizing studies in the Zitouna religious seminary and creating Sadiqi College (1875) "on the model of European lycees."[7] With his departure only a few chaotic years remained before French troops moved in from Algeria in 1881 to inaugurate the era of the Protectorate, destined to last until 1956.

BIN DIYAF'S *MUQADDIMA*: AN OUTLINE

Bin Diyaf opens his *Muqaddima* with the classic Muslim *bismallah*, "In the Name of God, the Merciful, the Compassionate." He then moves on in this first short section that serves as a preface to justify history "as one of the means to the sciences of the Religious Law." Interestingly, Ibn Khaldun began his *Muqaddima* by lauding history and even insisting that history "deserves to be a branch of philosophy."[8] Bin Diyaf consciously had in mind his fellow Tunisian of centuries past as a model, citing Ibn Khaldun first in his listing of Tunisian historians, including his contemporaries. Then Bin Diyaf outlines the contents of the entire *Ithaf*.

Following the preface is a short section entitled "On Government and its Varieties." Here Bin Diyaf presents the classic argument: Government is a necessity. Men acting alone cannot provide for all their needs. Men, however, will submit and cooperate only if held in check by a restraining power (*wazi*), this very term figuring prominently in Ibn Khaldun's *Muqaddima*.

The *wazi* is government, or, more explicitly, the ruler, for the rhetoric of Islamic political thought adheres to the concept of the single ruler, the monarch. That single ruler in mainstream Muslim political thought, which Bin Diyaf follows, is the Prophet Muhammad and, thereafter, one of his successors—the imam or caliph.

Bin Diyaf mentions, but rejects, the notion held by certain Muslim thinkers (for example Mu'tazilites and Kharijites) that the office of iman was not necessary. Moreover, as to whether the need for government can be established solely by use of human reason or stems from the teachings of Revelation, Bin Diyaf, again following mainstream Muslim doctrine, embraces the latter position. Yet, his few lines on this are not lacking in obscurity. He writes in a difficult-to-translate sentence (clarity in the Arabic having been sacrificed to rhyming prose): "What restrains oppression is either upbraiding reason (*ʿaql*) or restraining religion or deterring government or incapacity that turns one away from action." That is, the need for government as well as the proper rules for the conduct of government can be worked out by non-Muslims using human reason or by Muslims relying on Revelation. Or, best of all, implicit in Bin Diyaf's terse and elliptical text is the implication that Muslims have the advantage of deriving the proper role of government from a combination of reason and Revelation.

In any case, the issue becomes moot, since Bin Diyaf ends this section by accepting the doctrine (again, emphasized in Ibn Khaldun) that the true caliphate lasted only through the period of the first four "rightly-guided caliphs," Abu Bakr, ʿUmar, ʿUthman, and ʿAli, ruling from 632 to 661.

"Thereafter, only kingship [*mulk*] remained." Bin Diyaf's next three sections treat in sequence his idea of the three types of kingship—absolute rule, republican rule, and "rule limited by either Religious Law or political reason." In this latter definition, Bin Diyaf comes out clearly for what might be called the two roads to truth. Both reason and Revelation lead to the constitutional rule that he seeks.

Absolute Rule

Bin Diyaf needed few words to dismiss absolute rule as unjust and illegitimate. Absolute rule belongs only to God. It is sinful for a mere mortal to presume to such a prerogative. Even so, the notion that rulers must be obeyed is a bedrock Muslim principle: "O you who believe! Obey God. And obey the Messenger [Muhammad]. And those in authority among you." (Qur'an 4:59) Absolute rule is illegitimate, but should it be resisted? Is there a right of rebellion? Bin Diyaf takes his reader through a careful sifting of the various positions advanced by earlier scholars before concluding, again in line with mainstream Muslim thinking, that active resistance or rebellion is, in almost all cases, to be condemned. The danger that resistance might lead to disorder (*fitna*) in the community is so great that the oppressive ruler must be borne with patience.

Bin Diyaf cites a number of passages from Ibn Khaldun's *Muqaddima* to demonstrate the baleful effects of despotism on a people. With attacks on their property rights, exorbitant taxes, and debasement of coinage the people lose hope and interest in working and investing. As a result, civilization (*ʿumran*) declines. Nor is an amelioration to be expected from the fact that a despot, not matter how autocratic, must rely on ministers to carry out his will. Bin Diyaf bleakly noted that no such hopes could be forthcoming from such ministers who spend their time being sure that they stay on the right side of the ruler. They, as well, (here surely Bin Diyaf is using past accounts to evoke the contemporary infighting that afflicted the court he knew) engage in gossip and dubious schemes to undermine the standing of their fellow ministers.

Bin Diyaf, however, is not prepared to accept complete political quietism in confronting the absolute ruler. He cites a *hadith* of the Prophet as well as other stories to illustrate the high status granted individual believers who openly chastise the despot and suffer perhaps even death for their boldness. Such martyrdom is highly praised, but difficult to preach as a general guide for appropriate conduct. In any case, it would not easily jibe with the preferred stance of political quietism. Yet, without quite facing up to possible inconsistencies in his argument, Bin Diyaf does, along with citing approvingly these cases of martyrdom, evoke the basic Muslim principle of "commanding the good and forbidding the evil." One should speak out and reproach the unjust autocrat. At the very least one can and should "speak out" in the heart. "If you should follow past events in history books," Bin Diyaf insists, "you would see that changing evil by word often brings some effect and advantage."

So far, so good, but Bin Diyaf immediately adds, "We have never heard of any of the rulers who were great tyrants having punished by death or the like anyone who warned or advised or protested to him . . ." This is hardly consistent with the stories Bin Diyaf related of those martyred for doing just that or, for that matter, the story also cited by Bin Diyaf of the fate of the Barmakids.[9]

Republican Rule

In this short section Bin Diyaf notes that such rule prevails in "the country of America and others," but it is not right for Muslims. He cites the *hadith* of the Prophet Muhammad—"He who dies without allegiance (*bayʿa*) to an imam dies the death of the period of ignorance (*jahiliyya*)"— plus several other sources to assert that Islamic doctrine requires a single ruler. That ruler is the imam. Moreover, even though certain Europeans in earlier times erroneously dubbed Tunisia a "republic" (*mulk jumhuri*) they were mistaken. Tunisia has always been monarchical. Bin Diyaf then offers a brief review of Tunisia throughout the period of Islamic rule to substantiate his claim.

Even while dismissing republican rule as irrelevant to Muslims, Bin Diyaf offered this category of rule a very positive appraisal, largely in Islamic terms. With republican government the people choose their ruler. The person chosen is "like one of them" and he consults before taking action. Moreover, the people in republican rule possess laws "which they respect with the respect due the holy Shari'a type laws." It is a form of rule good for both the elite and the masses. It implements the Qur'anic injunction to consult, and Bin Diyaf cites the classic Qur'anic text—"their affairs are a matter of mutual consultation." (Qur'an 42:38).

Bin Diyaf's dismissal of republican rule as not acceptable for Muslims is based on two arguments, one normative and the other historical: (1) Islam requires governance by a single ruler, the imam/caliph. (2) Tunisia in the period since the arrival of Islam has always been governed by a single ruler.

As for Bin Diyaf's first argument, it is certainly true that a single ruler (the imam) governing a single Muslim community (the umma) provides a perdurable organizing framework for Islamic political thought, even to this day. Which is not to say that Muslim thinkers, past and present, have been blind to the reality of many different states governed by sultans and amirs, not caliphs. Major Muslim thinkers such as al-Ghazali, al-Mawardi, and Ibn Jama'a managed to formulate doctrines that papered over this reality of diverse, secular power wielders even while maintaining the formal ideal of a single imam/caliph ruling a single umma. It is not surprising that Bin Diyaf would embrace this ideal. As we have already noted and will have occasion to see throughout our description of his *Muqaddima*, Bin Diyaf in his political thought consistently adheres to prevailing Sunni Muslim orthodoxy.

Bin Diyaf's argument from history also leaves in place the concept of a single ruler. Even though the true caliphate gave way to kingship (*mulk)* when the last of the original four "rightly guided caliphs" was replaced by the Umayyad dynasty, that change left in place the notion of a monarch. Tunisia has, he points out, always had a single ruler even though often that single ruler operated under authority delegated from a higher sovereign, and in the case of Tunisia since the sixteenth century it is a matter of the Tunisian bey having "absolute authority by virtue of [Ottoman] sultanic delegation."

Bin Diyaf's firm rejection of republican rule as an option for Muslim countries would seem to legitimate, even if regretfully, the very autocracy that he would wish to see reined in. Why then would Bin Diyaf have bothered to evoke a form of rule little known at that time in the Middle East and little appreciated in either the Middle East or Europe? Perhaps there was some legacy in his thinking of the venerable tripartite classification, as old as Plato, of government by one, the few, or the many. Also the dialectic he sets up does offer a decided rhetorical flair. He presents first despotism, which is unacceptably bad, and then democracy, which has many fine points but is not allowed in Islam. Then he moves on to a more satisfactory new synthesis. The final sentence of this short section ringingly proclaims: "Thus, Tunisia's circumstances continued to deteriorate at times and even to come to a standstill until there appeared on Tunisia's horizon the first shimmerings of a constitutional dawn on Wednesday 14 Shallal 1277 [25 April 1861], and that is: governance limited by law [qanun]."

Governance limited by Law (Qanun)

This is the form of government, aside from the caliphate, "which shields the entire community and by which corruption is removed and on which the achievement of goals depends. The possessor of this type of rule is the shadow of God on earth, to whom the oppressed appeal and who heals wounds with his justice. This is because his rule is encircled by both reason and the Religious Law. The possessor of such authority conducts himself according to a well-known and reasonable rule that he never oversteps. He binds himself to thus act at the time of the oath of allegiance [bayᶜa], and he takes this oath before witnesses. If he acts so as to violate that oath then the agreement to obey him slips from the necks of the people."

Much meaning can be unpacked from this passage. First, although the true caliphate, Bin Diyaf is surely saying, is no more, it remains as an ideal against which governments are to be measured. Constitutional government (an appropriate adaptation of the literal "governance limited by law") is the best approximation of that ideal. Such a ruler has divine sanction. He is the "shadow of God on earth." There is hardly a better way to give this form of government the seal of approval than to link it to the caliphate.

Second, although the rubric "governance limited by law" could cover the entire gamut from monarchy to democracy, Bin Diyaf makes it crystal clear that he means a single ruler—the third person singular prevailing through this passage.

Third, by evoking both the Religious Law and reason as validating such a ruler, Bin Diyaf justifies borrowing from non-Muslims. That is, if Revelation is the necessary and sufficient guide to human conduct then it would be futile (perhaps even irreligious) to look to the experience of others. If, however, both Revelation and reason can serve as guides to human conduct then both not only can but should be used.

We have already seen Bin Diyaf wrestling with this Revelation/reason issue in asserting that the imamate was a necessity imposed by Revelation, not reason.[10] In doing so he opted, as was his wont, for the orthodox stance on this issue: Revelation requires the institution of the imamate. Even so, Bin Diyaf has kept the door open to human reasoning as a means, along with Revelation, for arriving at truth and proper conduct. That is surely the thrust of his earlier affirmation that oppression is reined in by either "upbraiding reason [ʿaql]" or "restraining religion."

Bin Diyaf comes close to saying, without denying the preeminence of Revelation, that both Muslims and others can achieve good government. What non-Muslims can arrive at using human reason is valid for this world. Muslims, using Revelation and reason, are able to institute a government valid for both this world and the next. That such is Bin Diyaf's purpose in yoking together Revelation and reason seems demonstrated in the next paragraph, wherein he avers that constitutional rule first appeared with the ancient Persians and "certain people of the Christian nation."[11]

A constitutional ruler takes the oath (bayʿa) before witnesses to obey such laws and if he violates that oath "the agreement to obey him slips from the necks of the people." In thus mentioning the bayʿa, along with calling such a ruler the "shadow of God on earth" Bin Diyaf has deftly added heft to the notion that a constitutional monarch comes closest to the religiously sanctioned caliphate. The *bayᶜa* ceremony is "comparable to the speeches of the rightly guided caliphs upon assuming office." By stating that if the monarch violates his oath the people are no longer bound by the agreement Bin Diyaf has advanced a powerful idea: Good government is based on a contract between the ruler and the ruled. To violate that contract renders it null and void.

Bin Diyaf's argument in favor of constitutional rule in this section is supported throughout by numerous approving references to the experience of non-Muslim Europe ranging in time from the age of the Byzantines, whose people were "most resistant to the tyranny of kings" to the reign of Louis Napoleon. Bin Diyaf, however, avoids saying, in effect, "we Muslims lack such institutions of government and must borrow from infidel Europe." Instead, he gives constitutional rule an Islamic pedigree.

The structure of his argument that Islam requires constitutional government is essentially as follows: Islam has a constitution. "The constitution of the Islamic government [*mulk*] is the majestic Qur'an and the sayings of the Messenger, may God bless him and grant him peace." This Qur'anic constitution gives mankind all the guidance needed for individual and group behavior. "We have left nothing out of the Book" (Qur'an 16:44). To stop at this point would logically rule out the need for a written constitution or, for that matter, any legislation (which as it happens is the orthodox position). It is all in "the Book." Still, even the pious and well-intentioned ruler, in his isolation, may misunderstand what is required in the public interest (*maslaha*). Or he may give way to his own willfulness. Therefore, he must consult. He must "heed the voice of those who command the good and forbid the evil." This is the way it was in the early days of Islam. In those days, the people and the preachers would call the rulers to account, but later rulers moved toward unrestrained autocracy.

Continuing to situate constitutionalism within Islamic orthodoxy, Bin Diyaf lauds Ottoman Sultan Sulayman (1520–66) who realized that "the domination of rulers did not stop at any limit and that circumstances were leading to the weakening of Islam." To remedy this situation the sultan known in the West as Sulayman the Magnificent but aptly called Sulayman the Lawgiver (*Qanuni*) in Ottoman and Muslim sources issued his famous *qanun*, which established a procedure by which the ʿulama' working with the Janissaries could hold the sultan to his commitments. This worked for a time, but then Islamic rulers lapsed yet again into absolutism. The needed new round of reform came during the reign of Sultan Mahmud II (1809–39) and was crowned early in the reign of his son and successor, ʿAbd al-Majid I (1839–69) with 1839 the *Hatt-ı Şerif* of *Gulhane* and the following age of reforms known as the *Tanzimat*. As if to underscore the importance of these Ottoman initiatives, Bin Diyaf provides a summary of Sultan Sulayman's *qanun* and the complete Arabic translation of the 1839 *Hatt-ı Şerif*.

An intriguing omission in Bin Diyaf's discussion of constitutional rule is any explicit reference to Tunisia's own experience with constitutionalism in the years from 1857 to 1864. After all, the title of his multivolume history refers not to the Ottoman Empire, not to Europe, not to forms of rule in general but to "the rulers of Tunisia and the Fundamental Pact." Yet, the Fundamental Pact (ʿAhd al-Aman) is not even mentioned in Bin Diyaf's *Muqaddima,* and there is only a single reference to the constitution promulgated in 1861. This is to be found in the concluding sentence in the chapter on republican rule, which ringingly proclaimed the appearance "on Tunisia's horizon the first shimmerings of a constitutional dawn on Wednesday 14 Shallal 1277 [25 April 1861]." Of course, a later volume of Bin Diyaf's history does record the story of Tunisian constitutionalism from 1857 on, in considerable detail (it is, indeed, the most thorough account available), and he includes there the full text of the ʿAhd al-Aman, which he himself composed.

Nor is Tunisia as such slighted in this chapter on constitutional rule. There are abundant references to Tunisia, especially the long disquisition about whether or not Tunisian rulers personally held court or delegated such juridical work to subordinates. Bin Diyaf also mentions his encounter with the eminent Ottoman scholar/statesman ʿArif Bey in 1842. He does not spare himself in relating his awkward attempt to defend Ahmad Bey's decision to "postpone" the implementation of the 1839 Ottoman Noble Rescript and ʿArif Bey's compelling defense of constitutionalism as being not only in accord with Islam but essential to Islamic governance properly understood.

Perhaps the answer to this omission is to be found in the circumstances prevailing when Bin Diyaf was writing his *Muqaddima*. The 1860s saw the imposing rural revolt that almost brought down the Husaynid dynasty and did lead to the suspension of the Tunisian constitution in 1864. That rebellion had denounced the constitution. This Tunisian denunciation of the new-fangled rules and the cry to return to the old ways mirrors precisely the situation in Ottoman Anatolia following the promulgation of the 1839 Noble Rescript as related by ʿArif Bey to Bin Diyaf. Incipient revolts in the countryside denounced these changes crying "the *Tanzimat* is a new religion. God's religion is Islam." ʿArif Bey, Bin Diyaf notes, received permission to visit the areas in revolt and explain the Islamic legitimacy of such constitutionalism, and he won over the populace. Reporting after his return, ʿArif Bey informed the sultan that he and his subjects will be delighted, and only those corrupt officials hiding behind the abuses of the bad old ways will be wretched.

By concentrating on the more positive developments in the Ottoman Empire (Bin Diyaf died two years before the short-lived Ottoman constitution was promulgated in 1876 only to be suspended in 1878) and by citing the story of ʿArif Bey that those opposing constitutional reform are either the misinformed masses or corrupt officials, Bin Diyaf could present his case in the best possible light. It might be noted that the other great Tunisian reformist treatise, that of Khayr al-Din, published in 1867, also avoids reference to the fate of the Tunisian constitution, concentrating instead on the Ottoman *Tanzimat*.

Immediately after his long narrative account concerning which Tunisian rulers held court and which delegated this judicial function to others, Bin Diyaf offers his most explicit account of European parliamentary government. These parliaments consist of a "consultative assembly composed of notables and the intellectuals of the state elected by the people. The composition of the assembly, the manner of electing its members, the conditions governing the elected and the electors and the number of its members may vary according to the conditions and customs of the countries." He then explains the concept of ministerial responsibility in a rather circuitous fashion. These assemblies are able not just to question ministers but even to demand their dismissal "should they take actions violating the constitution." He then explicitly says that such a demand really amounts to opposing the rulers themselves "but for this veil of propriety." This, he explains, is useful because representatives might well hesitate or fear to openly oppose the ruler, but they would feel less restricted in opposing or even demanding the dismissal of his minister.

A few lines later, however, Bin Diyaf reverses himself and asserts that "to oppose the minister—who is a delegate—is not like opposing the ruler." Why? Because the ruler is to the country like a father to his children. That ministers should be "reproached" is entirely appropriate. They "possess security and freedom just like the generality of the people, unlike those wretched ministers mentioned earlier in the first section on absolute rule caught between the lion's claw and the fang." Why do such ministers who might be reprimanded or even dismissed "possess security and freedom," unlike the fate of the Barmakids in the time of Harun al-Rashid or Tunisian officials such as Bin Diyaf's own father? Bin Diyaf does not elaborate on this point except to say that European constitutionalism resembles that of Sultan Sulayman, concluding that this is why there are few rebellions against rulers in Europe "because the ruler, if he ascertains from the assembly—which is the spokesman of the people— a disposition to rebel" he responds by "showing the restraint of a father to his son in order to avoid disobedience."

Immediately thereafter, Bin Diyaf takes another step to legitimate what he deems praiseworthy of European practice. Having compared European constitutionalism to Sultan Sulayman's great *qanun*, promulgated two centuries earlier, he asserts that such a European system is "worthy of esteem according to the Islamic Religious Law for it unifies opinion and avoids differences in the community, brings love between the ruler and the ruled, and spares bloodshed and wealth."[12]

Conclusion to the Muqaddima

Following discussion of this third, and clearly preferable, category of rule—constitutionalism—Bin Diyaf ends his *Muqaddima* with a short conclusion setting out an impressive selection of Qur'anic verses, *hadiths*, and maxims from Islamic wisdom literature (including the beautifully evocative advice that Hasan al-Basri is reported to have given the caliph ʿUmar ibn ʿAbd al-ʿAziz). Not at all a summation of the argument for constitutionalism, these concluding pages are simply a ringing exhortation to the ruler to rule with justice. As such, it fits the genre of "advice to kings" or "mirrors for princes" literature, which gives almost exclusive attention not to those ruled, not even to the "rules," but to the ruler. All of which is in keeping, as already noted more than once, with the mainstream literature of Islamic political thought—the idea of the good ruler ruling well. To those for whom Bin Diyaf wrote, this conclusion was surely a powerful homily, planting in a familiar Islamic soil the argument set out in his *Muqaddima*.

THE *MUQADDIMAS* COMPARED

Another way to situate Bin Diyaf's *Muqaddima* into its historical context is to compare it with that of Khayr al-Din. Since Khayr al-Din was the acknowledged leader of that small group of westernizing reformers in Tunisia, of which Bin Diyaf was an important member, the two *Muqaddimas* can be expected to advance similar arguments and strive for similar goals. That is certainly the case, but they offer interesting differences both of style and substance.

A first point to establish is the relative influence of the two at the time they were written and the years thereafter. Here, manifestly, Khayr al-Din's work outshines that of Bin Diyaf. *The Surest Path*, which appeared in 1867, was published not just in Arabic in 1867 but the following year in French (with a second French edition in 1875) and then in Turkish in 1878.[13] Khayr al-Din, himself, took the initiative in getting the French translation published, which underscores that his purpose in writing the book was to reach both European and Ottoman (including Tunisian) readers. The Turkish translation came just at the time Sultan ʿAbd al-Hamid invited Khayr al-Din to Istanbul and soon thereafter appointed him grand vizier.

Bin Diyaf's *Ithaf*, written in the years 1862–72, was not published until a century later. Available, thus, only in Arabic and in a small number of manuscript copies it was accessible to limited numbers, mostly Tunisians. There is, accordingly, a vast difference in the contemporary and even later impact of the two works. We should not, however, discount too much the accessibility of Bin Diyaf's *Ithaf* during those many years when it was available only in manuscript. Tunisia and, for that matter, the entire Muslim world, having lived for centuries with manuscript media, was in those latter decades of the nineteenth century still converting from manuscript to print. For example, most of the Tunisian historians cited in Ahmed Abdesselem's thorough study[14] remain to this day available only in manuscript or, as was the case of the *Ithaf,* had their works published only in the twentieth century. Tunisian scholars and opinion molders, the reading public, were in those years still accustomed to seeking out manuscripts just as they had been in centuries past.

Moreover, one very solid example of Bin Diyaf's influence can be cited. This is the book *Safwat al-Iᶜtibar bi Mustada' al-Amsar wa al-Aqtar* (The Essence of What Should be Known of Cities and Countries) by Shaykh Muhammad Bayram V (1840–89) scion of the eminent family of ᶜulama' whose members served in almost unbroken sequence as the Hanafi grand mufti or shaykh al-Islam in Tunisia from 1773 to 1861.[15] Published in 1884, not in Tunis but in Cairo, this work, as the title indicates, was something of an encyclopedic survey, but by far the longest and most important part treated Tunisia. The section just on Tunisian history to the establishment of the French Protectorate in 1881 accounts for 257 pages in the newly edited edition of the *Safwat*[16] and Bayram V acknowledges throughout the text that his principal sources were Bin Diyaf and Khayr al-Din, especially the former. This is not surprising. Bayram V was a younger member of the small group of Tunisian reformers.

Another obvious but relevant point to be made is the timing of the two *Muqaddimas*: Bin Diyaf was a member of Khayr al-Din's inner circle. He completed his *Ithaf* after the publication of *The Surest Path.* Thus, Bin Diyaf, while writing his history, had access to the published work of Khayr al-Din, and the notes accompanying our translation of Bin-Diyaf's *Muqaddima* reveal his numerous direct borrowings from Khayr al-Din. There is thus a clear sequential relationship between the two texts. As is often the case with the writings of those who can be said to form a "school" of political thought there is a master text written by the leader and subsequent texts by followers which are in large measure commentaries on the master text. By studying all such texts one can not only better see how the ideas of the master text were understood and interpreted at the time but can also trace the development of what we, in retrospect, single out as a distinctive "school" of thought. Bin Diyaf's

Muqaddima, seen from this perspective, becomes an important source for appraising Khayr al-Din's master text. The same can be said for the substantial Tunisian portions of Bayram V's *Safwat*, which would be an attractive subject for subsequent study.

Khayr al-Din's *The Surest Path* was, as noted, written for a dual readership, both Europe and the vast world of the Ottoman Empire. It is appropriate in this case to speak of the larger Ottoman world, not Tunisia. It is, indeed, striking the extent to which this political treatise, penned by an active statesman who spent almost his entire career involved in Tunisian politics, almost completely ignores Tunisia. The entire *Muqaddima* to *The Surest Path* includes only two references to Tunisia. In the first, Khayr al-Din, in explaining the purpose of his book, tells us that he was "fired to believe that if I assembled what years of thought and reflection had produced plus what I had seen during my travels to the various states of Europe where I had been sent by His Majesty the Bey, then my effort might not be without benefit, especially if it comes upon hearts working together for the defense of Islam." In the only other reference to Tunisia, Khayr al-Din does no more than cite the political treatise *Risala fi al-Siyasa al-Shar‘iyya* (Treatise on Governance according to the Religious Law) written by the Tunisian scholar Muhammad Bayram I (died 1800). That citation, however, has nothing to do with Tunisia as such. Bayram I was invoking earlier Muslim scholars in order to argue for a flexible interpretation of the Shari‘a that would permit adapting to changing circumstances.[17] Khayr al-Din makes no mention of Ahmad Bey's westernizing reforms, no mention of the 1857 ‘Ahd al-Aman, and provides not even a word about the short-lived constitution promulgated in 1861. The context of this political treatise was the Ottoman Empire on the one hand and Europe on the other.

Why did Khayr al-Din choose to thus ignore what he knew best—the case of Tunisia? Looking back now on his later career, in which he was summoned to Istanbul and even served for a short (alas, unsuccessful) period as grand vizier, it would seem plausible to assume that his personal interest transcended Tunisia to embrace the vaster Ottoman state. Still, it must surely be more to the point to suggest that Khayr al-Din was concerned about both Tunisia and the Ottoman Empire. While not unmindful that a constant concern of Tunisian beys in those years was a possible loss of Tunisian autonomy (direct Ottoman rule had been imposed on neighboring Libya in 1835) Khayr al-Din must have felt that confining his argument to examples from Ottoman experience (without explicit reference to Tunisia) better made his case for both the larger Ottoman Empire and the smaller Tunisia. By sticking to the Ottoman story and avoiding that of Tunisia he was able to skirt the delicate issue of whether Tunisia had a "right" to its autonomy (not to mention the possibility of even independence) or whether, on the other hand, Tunisia should become more closely tied to Istanbul (even abandoning its autonomy and accepting direct Ottoman administration). Second, writing a book published in 1867, Khayr al-Din was clearly haunted by the ill-fated Tunisian ventures in constitutionalism. The Tunisian constitution had been suspended following the traumatic revolt in the Tunisian countryside, a revolt that raised the cry against just such "reforms." It would not be easy to make a case for constitutionalism based on the Tunisian experience in the 1860s. Better to make the case for the Ottoman *Tanzimat* reforms, which could more plausibly be presented as a success story.

Differently stated, by addressing the Ottoman whole without reference to its several parts such as Tunisia (or, for that matter, Egypt) Khayr al-Din was able to present a single, general argument that was just as applicable as a model for those ruling in Tunis or Cairo as for the Ottoman rulers in Istanbul. The thematic unity of the single Ottoman whole also fit snugly into the framework of classical Islamic political thought, positing a single ruler governing a single community (*umma*), which also figured in Khayr al-Din's treatise.

Bin Diyaf , too, fitted his argument into an Ottoman framework, as noted in our discussion of his preferred polity "governance limited by law" (*qanum*).

As well as offering many, and favorable, references to the Ottoman experience, both Bin Diyaf and Khayr al-Din clothed their texts in a learned Islamic dress with citations from the Qur'an, the *hadith* literature and the works of the most eminent scholars of the classical Islamic period. Such an approach, both authors surely realized, was best for an argument intended for Muslim readers. To laud the actions of the last great Muslim polity, the Ottomans, and to build a case for consultation and constitutionalism as having impeccable Islamic credentials made it much easier to argue that Muslims must change with the times and must learn from infidel Europe. This approach presented in each *Muqaddima* has a coherence and relevance that could only have been assembled by someone well learned in the Islamic religious and cultural tradition. For a statesman of mamluk origins like Khayr al-Din this, in itself, would be a surprising feat. Not that Khayr al-Din was poorly educated. He had had a good education at the then newly created Bardo Military School (which included some religious studies) and thereafter made the most of his exposure to the world in the three languages he knew (Arabic, French, and Turkish) to become a cultured and learned man. Still, he did not have the kind of education that the ʿulama' and scribes such as Bin Diyaf received. It is generally accepted that Khayr al-Din relied on help from those ʿulama' and religious scholars who made up his small circle of followers in penning those passages. Indeed, *The Surest Path* seems to have been in many ways very much a team effort. Certainly, the many apt Islamic references were either written or at least carefully checked by one or more of the religiously learned.

Bin Diyaf's text, on the contrary, is certainly his work alone. Trained as a religious scholar (his father, be it remembered, had hoped he might join the ranks of the ʿulama' rather than the beylical bureaucracy) and then spending a lifetime as a writer in intimate contact with the community of religious scholars, Bin Diyaf was probably able to write scores of pages in a few hours without needing more than memory and his own working library readily at hand. That being the case, it is interesting to see the overlap of references and arguments taken from Islamic classics in the two *Muqaddimas*. This, in itself, illustrates what might be called the common corpus of Islamic learning shared by members of the religious and scholarly elite in Tunisia at that time.

A difference in depth and extent of coverage separates the two. Khayr al-Din's Islamic references, while able and apt, are fewer. Bin Diyaf offers more, and that more is presented more in the style of classic Islamic scholasticism. This involves, inter alia, reviewing all the disparate opinions on an issue before opting for one. Or perhaps, more cautiously, not even making a clear choice, observing simply that among scholars "there are differences." This is nicely seen in Bin Diyaf's wrestling with the issue of the right to resist unjust rulers in Islam. Or when Bin Diyaf, showing a good grasp of the rudiments of economics, praises the availability of developmental capital at low interest in Europe but then goes out of his way to insist that Islam categorically prohibits interest. It is as if Bin Diyaf is as much concerned to demonstrate the rich range of Islamic thought on this or that subject as he is to advance his argument.

In both *Muqaddimas,* Europe looms large. Indeed, somewhat more than half of Khayr al-Din's *Muqaddima* deals with Europe, and most of those pages are directly translated from European sources.[18] These include a full forty-one pages under the rubric "European Civilization" that must surely have come from one or several different European texts, but the precise source has not, as far as I know, been identified. Another passage of twelve pages is acknowledged to have been taken directly from two French scholarly sources.[19] These are not at all about Europe but, instead, relate the splendors of Islamic civilization at a time when Europe was in its "dark ages."[20] They are early examples of what became a common motif in Muslim writings thereafter—citing Western sources to prove the excellence of Muslim civilization at an earlier time, even its superiority over the West.

Not surprisingly, Bin Diyaf, with nothing like Khayr al-Din's experience of Europe and reading only Arabic sources, deals less with Europe. Indeed, several of his references to Europe are borrowed from discussions with Khayr al-Din or from *The Surest Path.*[21] Bin Diyaf cites, in addition to Khayr al-Din, as other sources for his knowledge of Europe the famous book by the Egyptian al-Tahtawi, recounting his years in France as "chaplain" to the Egyptian student mission sent there by Muhammad ʿAli and that semi-encyclopedia with the endless title that had been translated into Arabic and published in Cairo in 1833: G. B. Depping's *Evening Entertainment, or Delineations of the Manners and Customs of Various Nations interspersed with geographical notices, historical and biographical anecdotes, and descriptions in natural history designed for the instruction and amusement of youth* (1812). There was also Bin Diyaf's firsthand experience of Europe when he accompanied Ahmad Bey on his state visit to France in 1846.

Even with his limited experience, what Bin Diyaf has to say about Europe and Europeans is perceptive. With a commendable common sense he is able to see the strength of European venture capital and contrast it with the poor planning that plagued the Tunisian effort to install a rudimentary telegraph system. Admittedly, much of this is to be found in *The Surest Path,* but Bin Diyaf gets it right in his own words. His good understanding of economics, noted above, comes across even better by being stated in clear logical language available to the uninitiated. His picture of a Europe with banks that make capital accessible on easy credit, governments that do not debase their own coinage, and citizens with sufficient faith in governmental credit worthiness to subscribe to government loans amounts to an effective critique of the systemic failures in Tunisia that can readily be grasped by his readers.

Both Khayr al-Din and Bin Diyaf offer a consistently positive image of neighboring Europe. Indeed, both accounts come close to presenting almost idyllic accounts. The rulers are just, the people quick to oppose any infringements of their rights, their property is secure, the financial system sound, and because of this happy situation Europeans are actively engaged in increasing wealth and knowledge for all. Since our two authors represented a polity threatened by that same Europe, this sanguine appraisal of Islam's old neighbor and enemy needs explaining. When writing their books during the 1860s, they, themselves, had lived through such recent examples of European intervention as the wresting of Greece from the Ottoman Empire in the 1820s, capturing Algeria in the 1830s, and landing French troops in Lebanon in the 1860s. They knew, from first-hand experience, that virtually all major events in the larger Ottoman arena during these years were shaped by Europe. Even the very ʿAhd al-Aman that forms part of the title Bin Diyaf chose for his *Ithaf* was brought about by European intervention (which Bin Diyaf makes quite clear in his history even if he avoids mention of it in the *Muqaddima*). They also realized the strength of the Islamist and nativist forces that could be rallied (and had been rallied) against alien ways. This, surely, is why they presented an argument that linked current Ottoman and earlier Islamic practices to what a powerful Europe exemplified in their day.

Why, however, didn't Khayr al-Din and Bin Diyaf hedge their praise of things European? Or why didn't they in addition to asking "What went wrong?" also ask "Who did this to us?"[22] Wouldn't this have sweetened the bitter pill of borrowing from the alien, infidel Other? Since Khayr al-Din clearly had planned a book intended to reach at one and the same time a European and Ottoman readership, his praise for Europe (coupled with that long passage citing European praise of Islamic civilization in earlier times) is more understandable. In any case, Khayr al-Din does make a point of explicitly disengaging the religious issue. It was not, God forbid, that Christianity offered a greater worldly success than Islam. Indeed, the most retrograde political community in Europe was the Papal State. This was because of the Pope's "unwillingness to imitate the political ordering recognized in the rest of the European kingdoms" and Europe "had attained . . . progress in the sciences and industries through *Tanzimat* based on political justice."[23]

Bin Diyaf, writing only for his readers of Arabic, was even more outspoken in praise of Europe. This is most poignantly expressed in Bin Diyaf's citing the shocked reactions of Europeans who are "characterized by a longing to know about and understand things" to the parodies of justice performed in Tunisian courts of his time. Bin Diyaf's sense of shame for his government and his country in relating these incidents is palpable.

Does one then have to see Bin Diyaf as disaffected from his own religion, country and culture? Absolutely not. His love of both his religion and his *patrie* is clear throughout the *Ithaf*. Just as he cites more than once the image of the good ruler treating his subjects like a father kindly training and, as necessary, upbraiding his sons, so, too, does the family trope apply to him. Bin Diyaf may be seen as telling his "family" that, given their lofty pedigree as heirs to the once-great civilization of Islam, they ought to regain the standing they once held. That said, his obvious admiration of Europe is clear. There is not a hint of "who did this to us?"

Did Khayr al-Din and Bin Diyaf simply not see Europe as a clear and present danger? Albert Hourani, in his path-breaking *Arabic Thought in the Liberal Age, 1798–1939*,[24] has suggested as much. Tahtawi and Khayr al-Din (and by implication others of their generation) did not view the danger Europe posed as having become "so great as to constitute the central problem of political life, and the main problem was still what it had been for the Ottoman writers of the seventeenth and eighteenth centuries—internal decline, how to explain and how to arrest it." It was, Hourani continues, during the period 1875–82 (the disastrous 1875–78

Eastern crisis, the 1881 French Protectorate over Tunisia followed the next year by the British occupation of Egypt) that the European threat loomed large. There is much to be said for this interpretation, especially as regards Bin Diyaf. After all, up to the year when Bin Diyaf completed his *Ithaf*, European intervention had largely advanced the Tunisian reformist project. Indeed, perhaps yet another reason why Bin Diyaf did not dwell on the European intervention that made possible the ʿ*Ahd al-Aman* and the 1861 constitution in his *Muqaddima* was to avoid highlighting the foreign role. The continued diplomatic games pitting Britain and the Ottomans against France regarding Tunisia's status seemed to maintain the beylik's autonomous status. The existence of an alien French rule in Algeria should have caused greater concern, but then the many wars between Algeria and Tunisia during the Ottoman period, and the Tunisian concerns about its larger and stronger neighbor, made even that significant change seem perhaps unthreatening.

Whatever their reasons, neither Bin Diyaf nor Khayr al-Din offer even a whiff of the kind of anti-Western rhetoric that was later to prevail, and prevails to this day.

A Concluding Appraisal

Both the *Ithaf* and *The Surest Path* were produced during that short-lived "constitutional" period of Tunisia's history in the 1850s and 1860s. Both were programmatic statements intended to advance the cause of constitutional government. Looking at this period today, almost 150 years later, we have the luxury of hindsight that should make it easier for us to evaluate what these reformers were seeking. We can judge if they were successful. We can even perhaps gauge just how important they were not just in Tunisia but in the larger Ottoman world. Of course, in offering such post-facto appraisals, we must avoid the lure of making sense of the past in terms of the present.

The short-term answer concerning their success is easily made. Their goal of achieving a constitutional regime in Tunisia or elsewhere was not reached. Indeed, there is no little irony in that both of these works were completed *after* Tunisia's moves toward constitutional government had crashed on the rocks of the 1864 revolt. Then, after both works had been completed, Khayr al-Din returned to office in Tunis as prime minister during the years 1873 to 1877, but he made no effort to restore the constitution or to institute even the most modest form of institutionalized political representation. It is as if he had decided to concentrate on making government more just, more efficient. Government for the people now, government of and by the people postponed *sine die*.

Yet another irony remains concerning Khayr al-Din and constitutionalism. After having been ignominiously driven from office in Tunisia in 1877 he was later invited to Istanbul by none other than Sultan ʿAbd al-Hamid II. Not too long after his arrival he was appointed Ottoman grand vizier on 4 December 1878. He was not destined to last long. Envied by the Ottoman officials for his rapid rise from a provincial post to the top position in the empire, scorned as "that Arab"[25] he soon lost favor and was dismissed less than eight months later on 28 July 1879. The same Khayr al-Din, who had taken no steps to restore the constitution in Tunisia, and who arrived in Istanbul knowing full well that ʿAbd al-Hamid II had recently suspended the 1876 Ottoman constitution, proposed to the sultan the restoration of parliamentary life in the Ottoman Empire and the adoption of ministerial responsibility.

Thus, both constitutions were suspended after being operative for an almost equally short period of time. The Ottoman constitution was not restored until after the 1908 Young Turk revolution. The Tunisian constitution was never restored. Constitutionalism—and these two specific constitutions, Tunisian and Ottoman—did, however, remain a rallying cry for later liberals and reformers. In Tunisia, beginning in the first years after the establishment of the French Protectorate, a group of young proto-nationalists explicitly saw themselves as following in the tradition of the first generation of reformers. These were dubbed the "Young Tunisians."[26] Then, just after the end of the First World War, Tunisia's first nationalist movement was called the Destour Party. Why Destour (by that time the generally accepted Arabic term for constitution)?[27] The party was arguing that Tunisians deserved independence and had no need for French "protection." Tunisia, they maintained, had a "constitutional" past that should be restored.

In short, the political ideals expressed in these two texts produced roughly a century and a half ago were not institutionalized, but they did catch hold as a political philosophy influencing later developments. Bin Diyaf and Khayr al-Din contributed political ideas that have had an ongoing political life. They challenged what might be called the quietist tradition in Islamic political thought by presenting good government ruling over the good society as sanctioned by both religion and reason. They argued for not just the practicality but the religious duty of learning from others (thereby making palatable borrowings from a more successful Europe). They made the case for reining in the arbitrary ruler. In doing this, they reworked venerable Islamic ideas about consultation (*shura*), representation (*ahl al-hall wa al-ʿaqd*), and the oath of allegiance (*bayʿa*) as a virtual contract between ruler and ruled valid only so long as the terms are honored by both. The case for constitutionalism was also strengthened by their deftly blending Ottoman and European practice, thereby making the borrowing seem as much indigenous as it was foreign. A reorientation of political thought in Islam was presented as a recovery of the Islamic ideal. As such, the texts offer a living legacy.

Such is the larger historical context within which to situate Bin Diyaf and his *Muqaddima*. Stating the issue in this way may, however, tilt too much toward "presentmindedness." Seeing a moment of history on its own terms is a worthy exercise in itself. May this translation of Bin Diyaf's political treatise make us contemporaries of this eminent Tunisian and his times.

Ithaf Ahl al-Zaman bi Akhbar Muluk
Tunis wa ʿAhd al-Aman
[Muqaddima]

———————◆◆◆———————

Presenting Contemporaries the History
of the Rulers of Tunis and the
Fundamental Pact
Introduction

CHAPTER ONE

Invocation and Introduction

(1) In the Name of God, the Merciful, the Compassionate

Praise be to God, who created the heavens and the earth and produced darkness and light, the Examiner of hearts, the Controller of circumstances with the passing of epochs, the Knower of what eyes deceive and breasts hide. In His hand are the reins of the material and celestial worlds and to Him is resurrection. He makes the history of the predecessors a life for those in the grave and a light leading to the transmitted traditions, warning against the lures of harm and evil and awakening the minds from the slumber of vanity. I praise Him. He is to be praised and thanked. I bear witness that there is no God but God alone. He has no partner. This witness I bear for the day when debts are settled. I bear witness that our lord and master, Muhammad, is His servant and His messenger. He bears the hoisted banner of intercession. He has been sent with the Book, the balance and all-comprehending justice. He is confirmed by brilliant miracles and dominance, the guide to happiness by ordering what is required and forbidding what is forbidden. May God bless him and his family and his companions who drew from the sun of his prophethood the reinforcement of moons and substituted for him in his community by guiding it toward the purposes of the Religious Law[1] and the understanding of the recorded Book, and followed the interests of the people wherever that takes them, a permanent blessing with the permanence of the days and months.

(2) Thereafter, this poor creature in need of the Benefactor, Ahmad ibn Abi Diyaf, says:

The science of history, while numbered among the literary arts, is also one of the means to the sciences of the Religious Law. It helps one gain the proof of experience and it sharpens the thought of the learned and skillful, so that he can compare the cases of complaint and satisfaction to what happened in the past and see the causes and consequences as well as the events and what grows out of them.

But for history, the virtues would die out with the death of those possessing them. This would lead to their being ignored. The benefit is not disowned if the stories are told, the exceptional are tied down in writing, the deeds are transmitted, and the actions of those who did them remembered.

Such as the ruler who preferred, over personal interest, seeking what is right by planting good deeds and the means of welfare, whose concerns elevate him to rule the people. Whereas another was content with appearances and deemed anything permissible to such extent that his rule slipped away from him, leaving no beneficial deed and no favorable mention.

Or the vizier whose conduct was a model for the great ones. He will not be forgotten as time passes, but another will disappear without leaving a trace. The shimmering mirage deceived him, and he contributed only to the means of destruction.

Or the learned one who dominated the difficulties, mastered them, brought near their remoteness, and made obedient their stubbornness. He puts aside the rind to attain the marrow. He causes those of understanding to taste the sweetness of the Religious Law. He opens the most favorable door to treat the most constricted difficulties by means of religiously governed policy based on the public interest. As for the other, time made him a leader but he never moved his tongue for what would benefit. He was zealous to please the powerful and was unduly rigid in unnecessary matters, even if that led to the destruction of faith. He went to the presence of God with his deeds.

Or the writer who used his pen as a spear. He led the learned with the brilliance of his demonstration. He reached distant goals with his sharp arrows. The other, however, poured out ink only to mar the white paper with black filth.

Or the brave one, who ṣtrengthened preparedness and stood firm with the steadfastness of lofty mountains. He himself protected the religion, honor, and the homeland. The other only added to the number of the masses.

Or the generous, whose generosity has left great effect everywhere, and natures are disposed to him. Word about him pleases the ears. But the other is confined in his stinginess.

(3) Or the wise man in matters of religion, knowledge, and excellence. Ignorance to such as he is repulsive.

The science of history provides other advantages based on reason and supported by the transmitted texts. God Most High has said, "In their history is a lesson for those of understanding" (Qur'an 12:111). And God has said, "There has reached them news that should be a deterrence" (Qur'an 54:4). And He said, "They are those whom God guided, follow their guidance" (Qur'an 6:90).

The science of history provides other advantages for mankind of different religions, languages, and color, or different natural environments. Praise Him "Who taught by the pen, Who taught mankind what they did not know" (Qur'an 96:4–5).

A number of the eminent have concerned themselves with the history of this Tunisian *mamlaka,* may God increase its population and expand its resources, and of its rulers. These include Wali al-Din ibn Khaldun,[2] Abu ʿAbd Allah Muhammad ibn Ibrahim al-Zarakshi,[3] Abu ʿAbd Allah Muhammad ibn Abu al-Fadl al-Ruʿayni al-Qayrawani, known as Ibn Abu Dinar,[4] al-Wazir al-Saraj,[5] and others.

Also to be numbered in that rank is the learned vizier and scribe Abu Muhammad Hamuda ibn ʿAbd al-ʿAziz,[6] but his book is on the times of his master, Abu al-Hasan al-Pasha ʿAli Bey al-Husayni, as he pointed out in that book—and others are mentioned there passingly—and ends with ʿAli Pasha's reign. It is more like a panegyric.

After that, there was still history to be mentioned and events to be praised or blamed. Then our colleague, the eminent writer Abu ʿAbd Allah Muhammad al-Baji al-Mas'udi,[7] came forward and gathered what made a pleasant history and precious compilation that he entitled *al-Khulasa al-Naqiyya fi 'Umara' Ifriqiyya* (The Clear Epitome on the Rulers of *Ifriqiyya*). This goes up to the reign of the pride of the beylical house, of lofty reputation, the marshal and pasha Abu ʿAbbas Ahmad

Bey. He cites everyone in it, his famous deeds and whatever could be found in his history. This is done in a commendable and succinct style fashioned in an eloquence of pure gold.

The winds of the homeland moved me to write in a length that might well be considered good in this case, even though I am not in a class with these historians. Nor am I a knight in that domain. My youth is long past, my natural faculties exhausted and what power remains has been thrown off and become emptied. Still, my shortcomings may receive the approval and indulgence that the noble customarily extend.

(4) I have entitled this compilation *Ithaf Ahl al-Zaman bi Akhbar Muluk Tunis wa ʿAhd al-Aman* (Presenting the People of the Age with the History of the Rulers of Tunis and the Fundamental Pact). I have organized it into an introduction, eight chapters, and a conclusion.

The introduction contains two parts:

Part One is on the various types of kingship that exist. I conclude that with prophetic *hadiths* and wise sayings concerning justice and its opposite and what kings should do.[8]

The second part mentions only briefly the rulers of *Ifriqiyya* from among the companions of the Prophet, their followers and those who came after and also the royal dynasties in Qairawan, Mahdiyya, and Tunis, since information about them is related in earlier histories. I mentioned them only as a foundation and to complete the substance of this Introduction.

The following eight chapters treat each of the eight rulers of that number whose histories have not been written nor the stories about them assembled.

The first chapter records the reign of the unique in the string of jewels and the pride of the dynasty, Abu Muhammad Hammuda Pasha ibn al-Pasha ʿAli ibn al-Pasha Husayn ibn ʿAli, the founder of the dynasty.

The second chapter is on the reign of his half-brother on his father's side, Abu ʿAmr ʿUthman Bey.

The third chapter covers the reign of his paternal cousin, Abu al-Thina' Mahmud Bey ibn Abu ʿAbd Allah Muhammad Bey ibn Husayn Bey ibn ʿAli.

The fourth chapter is on the reign of his son, the well-loved ruler Abu ʿAbd Allah Pasha Husayn Bey.

Chapter 5 treats the reign of his full brother, the judicious ruler and ornament of the dynasty, Abu al-Nukhba Pasha Mustafa Bey.

Chapter 6 is on the reign of his son, the resolute and politic ruler, born to kingship, the Pasha and marshal Abu ʿAbbas Ahmad Bey.

Chapter 7 covers the reign of his paternal cousin, who proclaimed the Fundamental Pact (ʿAhd al-Aman) the marshal Pasha Abu ʿAbd Allah Muhammad Bey ibn Husayn Bey ibn Muhammad Bey, ibn Husayn Bey ibn ʿAli.

Chapter 8 is on the reign of his full brother, the present ruler, who proclaimed the constitution, the Pasha Marshall Abu ʿAbd Allah Muhammad al-Sadiq Bey.

(5) The conclusion offers what I was able to know of the biographies of certain of those ʿulama', viziers, scribes, and others of recent date. I mention only those who have been received into God's mercy. I list each group in the order of their death. The observer can know the history of those still living in the context of the subject treated. I have tried to do what was within my power to clarify the expressions used and bring them to understanding according to usage of speech, names, and titles current in the country.

I ask the help of God in His beneficence. He is the Ever Near, the Defender.

CHAPTER TWO

On Governance and Its Varieties

It is an accepted fact that government is a necessary condition for the human species and a necessity for the umma. Sunni Muslims acknowledge that the Religious Law requires this of the community. To fail to do this is a sin. It is one of the religious communal obligations[1]. Those of the community empowered to bind and loosen[2] are to choose the type of government.

Among the proofs that this is a necessity is the consensus of the companions of the Prophet, may God be pleased with them. This is because humans do not fulfill their existence in the course of ordinary life without banding together and cooperating on their essential needs. This is God's wisdom concerning His creatures.

The isolated individual cannot dispense with matters by which he ensures his life and without which life is not successful. There are many such things that he is not able to undertake without help from another. It is known that man cannot live without food and drink. Food comes into existence only by plowing, sowing, and reaping, and the use of tools for all these things. After the harvest come actions that it would take too long to enumerate. These things cannot be accomplished by one person. Man of necessity needs others for all of these activities and for what follows from them. This is the meaning of the saying "Man is civilized [*madani*] by nature." That is, his nature molds him to require communal life. (7)

As communal life takes place, necessity requires transactions and the fulfilling of needs. Each person extends his hand to what he needs according to his animal appetites, and the other restrains him according to his brute strength. This brings contention with strife, disorder, and bloodshed, leading to corruption of the species with which God has peopled His earth. This cannot be hidden. Therefore, God created a restrainer (*wazi*ᶜ) to stop the aggressor and with his protecting power give justice to the oppressed. Oppression is one of the ugly human defects. What restrains oppression is either upbraiding reason (*ᶜaql*) or restraining religion or deterring government or incapacity that turns one away from action.

Most men submit only to restraining power. "And if God had not repelled some men by others the earth would have been corrupted. But God is gracious to His creatures" (Qur'an 2:251).

Some scholars base the necessity of government on reason. They maintain that the resulting consensus is reached by the use of reason. They even hold that this is an obligation imposed on God, Himself, because to leave the people in anarchy and neglect is despicable.

"Some people have taken the exceptional position of stating that neither reason nor the Religious Law requires the office of an imam. People who have held that opinion include al-Asamm[3] from along the imams of the Muᶜtazilah and certain Kharijites. They think that it is necessary only to observe the religious rulings. When the umma agrees concerning justice and observance of the divine laws, no imam is needed, and an imam should not be appointed. They, however, are refuted by the general consensus. What drove them to such a doctrine was to escape the ways of government with its arrogance and mastery." This is what Ibn Khaldun has said in his *Muqaddima*.[4]

The correct opinion is that the necessity is imposed on the umma by the Religious Law, as discussed above. It is a bounty from God Most High. The conditions governing the incumbent of this post, which include knowledge, justice, and sufficiency, are fully detailed in the works on religious creeds and Islamic jurisprudence.

This restrainer is either a successor to the Prophet Muhammad or an ordinary ruler. The caliphate is intended to induce the people to follow the prescriptions of the Religious Law in their interest for this world and the world to come. According to the Lawgiver, all aspects of this world are linked to what is of benefit for the world to come. What is required of the (8) people is not just matters of this world, but their religious life leading to bliss in the world to come.

The period of the caliphate passed in accordance with the noble hadith, "The caliphate after me is for thirty years." It ended with the surrender of Hasan to Muʿawiya, may God be pleased with them. And this was one of the prophetic signs, for his grandfather, Muhammad, may God bless him and grant him peace, had said: "This son of mine is a sayyid. God will through him make peace between two great groups."

Thereafter only kingship [*mulk*] remained. It can be divided into three types: absolute rule, republican rule, and rule limited by either Religious Law or political reason.

CHAPTER THREE

Absolute Rule

(9) Such a rule can only be acknowledged for God, to Whom belongs all creation and authority, may God, Master of all, be praised.

The ruler of this type drives the people with his rod toward whatever he wishes of them according to his personal judgment of the public interest. He is not impeccable. He is just like other humans. Often, later rulers of this type have ruled just as they wished following their own passions, whether they accord with the public interest or not. At times they have even gone beyond the scope of reason, as was the case with the Fatimid al-Hakim in Egypt and those like him. They claim that they test in this way the limits of obedience from their subjects.

The people can be driven and led like grazing cattle, even though this leads to their harm and their being stripped of their prosperity, all through fear of his guards, whom he has made instruments for mastery and coercion. Certain subjects develop such a coloring of compliance and submission that they would not even think to themselves about opposing him. Nor would there stir in their hearts any deviation from obedience, so much have they been shaped with the passing years by the ignominy of exactions and coercion that has stripped them of the pride their fathers had and has effaced their self-respect. Moreover, the warnings in the Religious Law against disobeying those empowered to rule influence latterday people of the Islamic faith, who cleave to the apparent meaning of God's Word: "O you who believe! Obey God. And obey the Messenger. And those in authority among you" (Qur'an 4:59). Then, there are the words of the Prophet, may God bless him and grant him peace: "There will be imposed upon you rulers who will tyrannize. (10) God knows even more about them. If they act well they will have their reward and you should be thankful. If they act wrongly they will have their responsibility. You must be patient, unless they command infidelity [*kufr*], for there can be no obeying the creature who rebels against the Creator."

Al-Mawwaq,[1] in his book *Sunan al-Muhtadin* (The Traditions of the Rightly Guided), said: "al-Tartushi[2] has stated that the sultan is to be given what he demands even if that is unjust. He is not to be challenged." Ibn ʿAbd al-Barr,[3] in his Introduction [*Tamhid*] has said: "Certain of the Muʿtazilah and the generality of the Kharijites are of the opinion that the sultan is to be resisted in such cases.'

"Those possessing the truth [*ahl al-haqq*], that is those of the Sunna and the traditions of the Prophet and his companions, say that patience in obedience is worthier and more correct. The qadi al-ʿIyad[4] has said that all the *hadiths* of Muslim[5] are proof of this. As the Prophet, may God bless him and grant him peace, has stated, 'Obey them even though they take your possessions and strike you on your back.' Likewise, Ibn al-Munasif[6] has related on the authority of Malik, al-Shafiʿi, Abu Hanifa, and Ahmad ibn Hanbal, plus all those possessing religious knowledge that it is permitted for a man to fight, defending himself or his possessions or his people if there are those wishing to oppress him. Ibn al-Mundhir,[7] however, has retorted, 'Except against the sultan. If he is able to defend himself or his wealth only by rebellion against the sultan, then he must not rebel. This is because of the traditions commanding patience in the face of the tyranny and oppression that might come from the rulers and he should avoid fighting them.'" This ends the citation from al-Mawwaq.

You can see that the assertion of Ibn al-Mundhir is clear in insisting that a man can defend himself and his wealth against rulers but only by means other than rebellion. It is obvious that the ways of resistance other than rebellion or fighting are many, especially in these times. Injustice will lead to these measures. Indeed, the Noble Rescript,[8] to be mentioned later, refers to this.

Is the command to be patient a recommended or obligatory religious duty?[9] Certainly, patience is worthier, since wars bring bloodshed against which the angels in heaven cry out, raising their voices to God Most High: "Will You place there on earth one who will do harm and shed blood?" (Qur'an 2:30). This is especially the case if the wars are within a single community bound together by the brotherhood of religion and homeland. Such is a much more severe harm than the tyranny of rulers.

Ibn °Abd al-Barr has related that °Ali ibn Abi Talib, may God be pleased with him, said: "A just ruler is better than a downpour of rain. A destructive lion is better than an oppressive ruler. But an oppressive ruler is better than continuing civil strife [*fitna*]." (11) Think of the wars that took place in the early days of Islam and what resulted from them.

The Imam Malik, may God be pleased with him, avoids giving a fatwa calling for the support of such rulers against those resisting them. The learned al-Fasi[10] in his book a*l-Taysir wa al-Tashil fi ma Aghfalahu al-Shaykh Khalil* (The Easy and the Quick of what Shaykh Khalil did Overlook) reports the following:

> Ibn Yunus said, "Fighting the Kharijites is a religious duty." Then, later in the discussion he said, "Even if they are going after an oppressive ruler, you are not permitted to repudiate him or to rise up against him. You are not permitted to refrain from supporting the just regardless of whether he is the one in revolt or the unjust ruler against whom one is revolting."[11] Qadi al-°Iyad, citing al-Harith ibn Miskin,[12] said, "Certain rulers asked him concerning his fighting against some Kharijites," and he replied, "Ibn al-Qasim told me what he had heard from al-Malik that Harun al-Rashid asked him about such a case, and he replied 'If they have revolted because of the sultan's oppression, then fighting them is not permitted.'"

This ends al-Fasi's words.

Shaykh Halulu, in the commentary on a*l-Mukhtasar* (The Abridgement) has said: "Regarding one who rose against an imam trying to strip him of his rule, Ibn Yunus mentioned from the account of °Isa from Ibn al-Qasim from Malik that if the imam were someone such as °Umar ibn °Abd al-°Aziz,[13] then it is the people's religious duty to defend him and to rise up with him in resisting rebellion, but not for other rulers. The meaning of this is that God takes revenge against the oppressor by means of another oppressor. Then, He will take his revenge against both." This ends the citation. From this it is clear that the command of patience against the oppressive ruler is a recommended religious duty, but not obligatory.

Al-Hafiz ibn Hajar[14] relates that a Umayyad prince asked one of the Followers, "Didn't God command you to obey me by saying 'and those in authority among you?'"[15] He replied, "Are you not stripped of the right to be obeyed when you violate what is religiously true and right according to the words of God, 'And if you have a dispute concerning any matter, refer it to God and to the Messenger'" (Qur'an 4:59). Al-Tibi[16] and others have said, "Repeating the verb in God's command, 'And obey the Prophet,' indicates that the Prophet is to be obeyed unconditionally. That verb not being repeated for 'those in authority' is a way of stating that there would be some rulers to whom obedience is not due. Thus, God made this clear in His words, 'If you have a dispute concerning any matter, refer it to God and to the Prophet'" (Qur'an 4:59).

Most of the early Muslims have held that the binding force of the imamate was loosened with the nonfulfillment of its purpose, which was justice and restraining the hand of aggression, for if the ruler oversteps and violates the purpose for which he was put in office then he is not to be numbered among the imams.

(12) The shaykh of our shaykhs, Imam Abu Muhammad Hasan al-Sharif,[17] has said in his gloss on the *Commentary* of Shaykh Mayyara[18] on the *Lamiyya* of al-Zaqqaq[19] what can be summarized as follows: "The qadi ʿIyad said, 'There was disagreement at first. Later it was agreed that the people should not rise against rulers. Ibn ʿAbd al-Barr took the same approach in *al-Istidhkar*[20] in commenting on the passage "And no one should dispute people of authority" as follows:

> People disagree about this. Some say "people of authority" are those possessing justice, charity, virtue, and religion with the ability to undertake all this. These people should not be disputed, because they are those qualified for authority. As for those characterized by sinfulness and oppression, they are not so qualified. They support their argument by citing the words of God, All Powerful and Lofty, to Abraham, May God's prayers be upon him, "I made you an imam to the people." And Abraham asked, "And to my descendants?" To which God replied, "My covenant does not extend to

oppressors" (Qur'an 2:124). A group of the noble ancestors (al-Salaf) held this view, and virtuous successors from among the ʿulama' and fuqaha of Madina and Iraq followed them. This was why Ibn Zubayr and al-Hasan ibn ʿAli, may God be pleased with them, rose in revolt against Yazid ibn Muʿawiya, and the best of the people of Iraq as well as their ʿulama' rose against al-Hajjaj ibn Yusuf, and the people of Madina against the Umayyads. In these days, however, the Sunnis and their imams take the position that patience in the face of the tyrannical ruler is preferable to revolt. This is because resistance to him involves replacing security with fear, bloodshed, and corruption in the land, all of which is worse that patience before the tyranny of the tyrant.

Patience, however, does not exclude censure of such oppression, which is an obligation according to the Qur'an, the Sunna, and the consensus of the community (ijmaʿ). This is because the obligation to command the good and forbid the evil is one of the pillars of Islam and its very essence. To the Sunni Muslims this is a duty imposed by Revelation. To the Muʿtazilah it is imposed by reason according to conditions mentioned by those possessing religious knowledge (ahl al-ʿilm). Indeed, al-Ghazali said, "The person undertaking this does not need to be a practicing [Muslim] himself, for he is bound by two religious duties—to exercise self-restraint and to admonish others." Whosoever wants to become acquainted with that subject and its procedures has only to consult his Ihya 'Ulum al-Din (The Resurrection of Religious Thought), for he treats the matter at length.

If it is asked, did not God say, "O you who believe, you are responsible only for yourselves. He who strays does not harm you if you are rightly guided" (Qur'an 5:105), it can be answered that the meaning of the verse according to eminent scholars is that if you have complied then you are not harmed by the shortcomings of others who do not comply.

(13) It is mentioned in the book Taysir al-wusul ila Jamiʿ al-Usul min Hadith al-Rasul (Easing the Path to the Collection of the Sources of the Sayings of the Prophet)[21] that Abu Bakr, may God be pleased with him, said after praising God and extolling Him, "O people, you read this verse, 'O you who believe, you are responsible only for yourselves. He who strays does not harm you if you are rightly guided' and misinterpret

it. I heard from the Prophet of God, may God bless him and grant him peace, 'If people see an oppressor and do not take him by the hand to stop him then God will hasten to punish all of them.' Abu Daud and al-Tirmidhi have reported this."

The author of al-ʿIqd al-Farid (The Unique Necklace)²² relates one of the speeches of ʿUmar ibn al-Khattab, may God be pleased with him: "O people, fear God in your secret thoughts and in your public utterances, and command the good and forbid the evil. Do not be like the people in a boat in which one of them began to bore a hole. Others saw what he was doing and stopped him. He retorted, 'This is my place and I have control of it.' Now, if they were to still his hand both he and they would be saved, but if they were to leave him alone then he would be destroyed and they with him. This is a parable that I have drawn for you. May God have mercy on me and on you." And the Prophet, may God bless him and grant him peace, also said, "You must surely command the good and forbid the evil lest God hasten to send upon you a punishment at which time you will call upon Him but He will not answer."

And the Prophet, may God bless him and grant him peace, said, "Protect your brother whether he be an oppressor or oppressed." Then, he was asked, "I would protect him if he were oppressed, but how could I protect him if he were an oppressor?" The Prophet answered, "Hold him back from oppression. That would protect him." Al-Bukhari has reported this.

The Prophet, may God bless him and grant him peace, has said, "The most virtuous jihad is a word of truth before the tyrannical sultan."

Abu ʿUbaydah ibn al-Jarrah, May God be pleased with him, said, "O Prophet of God, which of the martyrs are most precious to God, the most Powerful and Lofty?" The Prophet responded, "The man who came before the tyrannical governor, commanded him to do the good and admonished him to abstain from evil, and the ruler killed him. If he had not killed him, the pen of the recording angel would not write about him however he might have lived thereafter."

Hasan al-Basri, May God have mercy on him, said: "The Prophet, may God bless him and grant him peace, said, 'The best martyr of my community is the man who stood before the tyrannical imam and commanded him to do the good and enjoin the evil, and the imam killed him for that. The standing of that martyr in heaven is between Hamza and Ja{c}far." And the Prophet, may God bless him and grant him peace, has said, "The best of the martyrs is Hamza ibn {c}Abd al-Muttalib, and then the man who stood up to the imam, commanded and admonished him concerning the things of God Most High, and the imam killed him for that." There are other such *hadiths* of the Prophet and verses of the Qur'an well established in the religious books.

(14) In the *Jami{c} al-Dhakhira* of Shihab al-Qarafi[23] is a section entitled "The question of the punishment of all for the sins of some."

And in *Muwatta{c}* (The Smoothed Way), Umm Salma asked, "O Prophet of God, will we perish while we have the virtuous among us?" He answered, "Yes, if there is great wickedness." God, Most High, has said, "Guard yourselves against a chastisement that will fall not only on those of you who are wrong-doers" (Qur'an 8:25).

Yet, going against these texts are the words of God, Most High, "No one bears the burden of another" (Qur'an 6:165), as well as His words, "He who strays does not harm you if you are rightly guided" (Qur'an 5:105).

The author of *al-Qabas*[24] said, "The punishment will spread [to the other person] if the one who abstains from evil acts does not admonish the one who does evil." Ibn {c}Abbas also said this, so the texts are in agreement. This is the meaning of God's words, "they do not restrain one another from the evil they did" (Qur'an 5:79).

His words "and does not admonish the one who does evil" refer to admonition even done only in the heart when one is unable to do otherwise. That, however, is the weakest of faith.

Consider the *hadiths* that threaten God's punishment for inaction in the face of evil. You find them among the signs of prophecy. For we have seen places in which not even the slightest action to change evil occurs, and they are not free of tyranny, corruption, deficiency, and other harmful things. "If harm touches a man he calls to his Master, turning to Him in penitence" (Qur'an 39:8). This is according to the Islamic disposition.

We have seen preachers in the houses of God, and among the most upright, pray humbly to God with the cry every Friday to correct the conditions of princes, dispel the anxieties of the Muslims, open the doors to the good, close the doors to evil, and other such prayers. Yet, we do not see these prayers ever answered in this world. This is only because of the lack of an effort to change evil, as was mentioned earlier in the noble *hadith* of the most truthful, may God bless him and grant him peace, when he said, "Then you will call to God and He will not answer you."

We have also seen that the people, both in the past and the present, are able to try to change evil by word, if they give up their zest for the pleasures of this world out of their love for rank, dignity, wealth, and other such aims.

Seeking to change evil by word does not require refusing obedience or rebellion against rulers by forming groups to resist. Changing evil by word has many different faces, and possibilities are available, such as sermons by the ʿulamaʾ, the heirs of the prophets, and the complaints of those oppressed presented without (15) undue harshness, improper behavior or discord, plus other such acts to defend against harm and take preventive measures. There is no doubt that all of this can result in some part of what is sought, and that which does not attain all still does not leave all behind.

If you should follow past events in history books you would see that changing evil by word often brings some effect and advantage. We have never heard of any of the rulers who were great tyrants having punished by death or the like anyone who warned or advised or protested to him, such as would make permissible abandoning this religious duty. Indeed, certain rulers of this sort, such as the Abbasids in the first period of their reign, had appointed a person to undertake this duty whom they call the holder of the *hisba* (*Sahib al-Hisba*) as a way of fulfilling the communal religious obligation lest they might be held to account by God for not doing so. In these recent centuries, however, the best people, that is the ʿulamaʾ, have put aside this religious duty for reasons that only God knows. They have forgotten this religious duty or have ignored mentioning it to such extent that Sultan Sulayman had to call it to their attention, as will be seen later.[25] Abandoning that duty is the reason for the weakness of Muslims and the decline of their countries, which is there for the eye to see.

Thus, absolute rule violates the Religious Law, because it capriciously treats God's creatures and God's land. The Religious Laws came to release the responsible person (*mukallaf*) from the exigencies of his desires. God Most High said to His Prophet; "O David! we have made you a vice-regent (*khalifa*; caliph) on the earth. Therefore judge aright between men. And do not follow desire, lest it beguile you from the way of God. Those who wander from the way of God have an awful doom" (Qur'an 38:26). Consider this warning. And the Most High also said, "And if the Truth had followed their desires, truly the heavens and earth and all therein would have been corrupted" (Qur'an 23:71). And the Most High also said, "And who goes farther astray than he who follows his lust without guidance from God? God does not guide the wrongdoers" (Qur'an 28:50). Other such verses of the Qur'an censure personal desires.

Ibn ʿAbbas,[26] may God be pleased with him, said, "God never mentions human caprice in His Book without censuring it." For this reason the Lawgiver in the above *hadiths* labeled it "tyranny, oppression, and injustice" and placed upon whomever engages in this the burden of guilt. God does not love oppressors or aggressors. It is said in the noble *hadith*, "The most wretched ruler is he who makes his subject wretched."

(16) Absolute rule is also opposed by reason, because it consists of mastery and coercion, both effects of wrath resulting from usurpation and brute force. The object of the restrainer is, as has been said, to provide equal treatment, eliminate aggression, achieve the public interest (*maslaha*), and avert corruption. How then can one who has been put into his position to get rid of oppression be himself an oppressor? A bedouin said to one such ruler: "You are given authority to look after us. Now you are eating us like a wolf. What are you, a wolf or a shepherd?"

This is the reason for the great number of those in revolt or resisting absolute rulers. Because the subjects become corrupted, rebelliousness is naturally found hidden within them as fire hides in the kindling, breaking out at the slightest stirring. Human nature finds it oppressive to bear harm. It awaits the opportunity to be rid of it, just as the slave awaits his emancipation. How few are those who have taken on the preferable temperament of patience. The natural disposition, however, can win out over the acquired and the real Muslims among them have in their hearts resentment to this evil, as is their religious duty. It is enough for them to pray against the unjust ruler and censure them because there is no religious problem with censuring the unjust imam as the guardian of the

Madhhab, Ibn Rushd, said in his *Muqaddimat.*[27] How then can the situation be made stable for a community whose people realize that their lives and their wealth are in the hands of one person? He can act as he wishes, not as would be wished of him. Nor will he be questioned concerning this, except in the world to come. In such circumstances they are in danger and trouble, given the differences in the human condition. From among these rulers there may be one who is just, another tyrannical, one clever, another stupid, one deliberate, another hasty, one severe, another lenient, one generous, another miserly, one wasteful, another economical, one prudent, another foolish, one proud, another modest, and other such differences as are found in human dispositions. This is God's wisdom concerning his creatures: "And had God so wished, He could have brought them all together in guidance" (Qur'an 6:35).

The effect of these differences appears among the subjects, for they lack a fixed, well-preserved nature. Instead, their nature changes with the change of rulers, rather like a domesticated animal, which at times may be happy with a gentle owner who looks after his interest and does not impose tasks upon him beyond his capacity, but at other times may be made wretched by a master who is severe with him and may even impose on him tasks that bring about his ruin. When danger appears, security disappears, and the disappearance of security brings the disappearance of hope, and with the disappearance of hope, work disappears. The fearful has no hope except in fleeing from oppression with his life and his wealth. That brings about the destruction of civilization (*'umran*).

Ibn Khaldun, in the chapter entitled "Injustice brings about the Ruin of Civilization" in his *Muqaddima*[28] has written: (17)

> It should be known that attacks on people's property remove the incentive to acquire and gain property. People, then, become of the opinion that the purpose and ultimate destiny of acquiring property is to have it taken away from them. When the incentive to acquire and obtain property is gone, people no longer make efforts to acquire any.
>
> The extent and degree to which property rights are infringed determines the extent and degree to which the efforts of the subjects to acquire property slacken. When attacks on property are extensive and general, extending to all means of making a living, business

inactivity, too, becomes general, because the general extent of such attacks upon property means a general destruction of the incentive to do business. If the attacks upon property are but slight, the stoppage of gainful activity is correspondingly slight.

Civilization and its well-being as well as business prosperity depend on productivity and people's efforts in all directions in their own interest and profit.

When people no longer do business in order to make a living, and when they cease all gainful activity, the business of civilization slumps, and everything decays. People scatter everywhere in search of sustenance, to places outside the jurisdiction of their present government. The population of the particular region becomes reduced. Its residences are emptied and its cities lie in ruins. The disintegration of civilization causes the disintegration of status of dynasty and ruler, because their peculiar status constitutes the form of civilization and the form necessarily decays when its matter decays. . . .

In this connection, one should disregard the fact that dynasties centered in great cities often infringe upon justice and still are not ruined. It should be known that this is the result of a relationship that exists between such infringements and the situation of the urban population. When a city is large and densely populated and unlimited in the variety of its conditions, the loss it suffers from hostile acts and injustice is small, because such losses take place gradually. Because of the great variety of conditions and the manifold productivity of a particular city, any loss may remain concealed. Its consequences will become visible only after some time. ...

The proven fact is that civilization inevitably suffers losses through injustice and hostile acts, as we have mentioned, and it is the dynasty that suffers therefrom.

Injustice should not be understood to imply only the confiscation of money or other property from the owners without compensation and without cause. It is commonly understood in that way, but it is something more general than that. Whoever takes someone's property, or uses him for forced labor, or presses an unjustified claim against him, or imposes upon him a duty not required by the Religious Law, does an injustice to that particular person. ...

It should be known that this is what the Lawgiver actually had in mind when he forbade injustice. He meant the resulting destruction and ruin of civilization, which ultimately permits the eradication of the human species. This is what the (18) Religious Law quite generally and wisely aims at in emphasizing five things as necessary: the preservation of (1) the religion, (2) the soul (life), (3) the intellect, (4) progeny, and (5) property.

Since, as we have seen, injustice causes the eradication of the human species by leading to the ruin of civilization, it contains in itself a good reason for being prohibited. Consequently, it is important that it be forbidden. There is ample evidence for that in the Qur'an and the Sunnah. It is much too ample to have it accurately or fully presented here.

If injustice were to be committed by every individual, the list of deterring punishments that would then have been given for it (in the Religious Law) would be as large as that given for the other crimes that lead to the destruction of the human species and that everyone is capable of committing, such as adultery, murder, and drunkenness. Injustice, however, can be committed only by persons who cannot be touched, only by persons who have power and authority. Therefore, injustice has been very much censured, and repeated threats against it have been expressed in the hope that perhaps the persons who are able to commit injustice will find a restraining influence in themselves. "Your Lord does not do injustice to His servants" (Qur'an 41:46).

It should not be objected that punishment for highway robbery is provided for in the Religious Law, and that highway robbery is an injustice that can be committed only by someone who has the ability to commit it, inasmuch as the highway robber, when he commits the robbery, must have the ability to do it. ...

It may be said that the highway robber cannot be described as having the ability to commit injustice, because we understand by ability to commit injustice that the person has a free hand and there is no rival power, which means that he has a power to bring about complete ruin. The ability of the highway robber is merely an ability to cause fear. This fear then enables the highway robber to take away the property of others. Everyone may defend himself against it, according to both the religious and the political law. It is not, then, an ability that could bring about complete ruin.

And then Ibn Khaldun added:

One of the greatest injustices and one that contributes most to the destruction of civilization is the unjustified imposition of tasks and the use of the subjects for forced labor. This is so because labor belongs to the things that constitute capital. Gain and sustenance represent the value realized from labor among civilized people. All their efforts and all their labors are means for them to acquire capital and to make a profit. They have no other way to make a profit except through labor. ...

Now, if they are obliged to work outside their own field and are used for forced labor unrelated to their ordinary ways of making a living, they no longer have any profit and are thus deprived of the price of their labor, which is their capital asset. Hardships befall them. ... The disintegration comes about gradually and imperceptibly.

This happens whenever the ways and means of seizing property described above are used. On the other hand, if the property is taken outright and if the hostile acts are extended to affect the property, the wives, the lives, the skins, and the honor of people, it will lead to sudden disintegration and decay and the quick destruction of the dynasty. It will result in disturbances leading to complete destruction.

This ends the gist of this section from Ibn Khaldun.

What has been set out above reveals the true nature of the religious sanction to forbid evil. It is a duty and those killed for its sake are martyrs.

(19) This wrongdoing is at times confined to a few individuals and at times extends to all the people. Examples include excessive taxes and levies on commerce in necessities such as food and the means of processing food, plus such essentials as fruit.

But the greatest harm and the most severe danger is the debasement in coins of the two noble metals—gold and silver—which God made to set the value of everything. Around its two axes revolve all transactions in the world.

The first to coin a spurious dirham in Islam was ʿUbayd Allah ibn Ziyad ibn Abi Sufyan, the killer of Husayn ibn ʿAli, may God be pleased with them both. Al-Suyuti relates this in his *Awwaliyat* (The First Things).

Ibn Khaldun, in discussing coinage in his *Muqaddima* has said[29]:

It is an office that is necessary to the royal authority, for it enables people to distinguish between good and bad coins in their transactions. That the coins are not bad is guaranteed by the engravings known to have been stamped upon them by the ruler.

The non-Arabs used coins and engraved special pictures on them, for example, a picture of the ruler at the time of issue, a fortress, some animal or product, or something else. This remained the practice of the non-Arabs down to the end of their power. When Islam appeared, the practice was discontinued, because of the simplicity of Islam and the bedouin attitude of the Arabs. In their transactions, they used gold and silver according to weight. They also had Persian dinars and dirhams. They used them, too, according to weight, and employed them as their medium of exchange. The government paid no attention to the matter. As a result, the frauds practiced with dinars and dirhams eventually became very serious.

According to the reports of Sa'id ibn al-Musayab and Abu al-Zinad, 'Abd al-Malik ordered al-Hajjaj to coin dirhams, and bad coins began to be distinguished from the good ones. This took place in 74 [693–94] or, according to al-Mada'ini, in 75 [694–95]. In the year 76 [695–96] 'Abd al-Malik ordered that dirhams be coined in all the other regions. The legend upon them was: "God is one, God is the Eternal" (Qur'an 112:1–2).

This ends the passage from Ibn Khaldun.

You can see from this context that inscriptions on the coinage are an attestation from the sultan that the coinage is free of debasement. And if the sultan mixed the coinage with other metals and then inscribed on them his name there would be snatched away from the people the profit they possessed, (20) to the extent of the debasement. All this would happen without the people, trusting in the ruler's inscription attesting to the soundness, being aware of what was happening.

Despotic rulers consider coinage a commodity for making profit whenever they feel the need to exercise the arts of excess in luxury. The most ignorant among them even exclaim, "Only the ruler may trade in coinage." They are rigorous in punishing those who might join them in such fraudulent trading. This is among the most imposing of reasons for the weakening of civilization and the destruction of cities and states in

Islam, especially whenever they are engaged in trade with European cities, because the European cities are extremely strict concerning the fineness of their coinage bearing the images of their rulers as witness to their purity. They only take into consideration the necessary expenses for striking the coins. They deem themselves above such profiting which would, as they see it, decrease the prosperity of their kingdoms. Their merchants respect only their own coinage. Knowing the debasement of the Muslim coinage, they recognize only that which is pure. Thus, in their view, consistent with divine wisdom the debased "passes away as scum."[30] For the Proof of Islam, al-Ghazali, said in his chapter on patience and gratitude in *Ihya 'Ulum al-Din* (The Revivification of the Sciences of Religion), as summarized:

> The creation of the dirham and the dinar is among the bounties of God Most High, for the world is based on them. They are two metals of no benefit in themselves. Yet, mankind needs them both. Since every man needs great support in securing his food, his clothing, and all of his needs, God created the dirhams and dinars as the two judges mediating among all kinds of wealth to such extent that everything is valued according to these two. The other virtue of these two is as a means toward all things, for they are precious in themselves and thus need no outside support. They fix the standard of value for all other forms of wealth. Thus whosoever owns them, it is as if he owns everything. Therefore, God warned against hoarding them or using them in any way other than as God intended.

This concludes the paraphrased summary of al-Ghazali's statement. Thus, you can see how the bountifulness of God Most High in granting these two coins and God's wisdom concerning them and the injunction of the Religious Law against their being hoarded or used in any way other than as commanded has become a plaything of despotic rulers, who sully the honor of these two coins with base coinage. All of this increases the disputes concerning the religiously authorized dirham and dinar upon which are based Religious Legal rulings on such matters as alms-giving, dowries, and the canonical punishments. The noble *hadith* exclaims, "He who cheats us is not one of us." Often these rulers mint copper coins and give them any evaluation based on silver that they wish in accordance with however much they want to gain wrongly. They increase such debased coins to a burdensome extent, leading to the destruction of business. The Europeans strike what they need of this debased coinage, but do not give it a value beyond what is spent on its being coined.

(21) From such as this it is revealed that the aggression of despotism causes the lack of prosperity and the destruction of cities. The evidence for this is the current situation and there is no argument stronger than that.

Look at the bedouin in their tents, how they turn away from building houses and planting trees and living close to water even though they know that such would be better than what they have of toil and discomfort in their lives, living among vipers. This can be appreciated by anyone capable of distinguishing a date from a live coal. The bedouin have been molded by this savagery, so contradictory to prosperity to such extent that they boast of it before the people of the villages and the cities. All this is to be accounted for by insecurity and the fear of attack. For this reason they are ready to flee. Those who from aversion to harm penetrate most deeply into the desert do not take with them sheep or cattle or the like. That would hinder them from getting into the innermost parts of the desert or the wasteland should they need to do that, escaping the oppression of the governor or other officials. A recent ruler of this sort gave free rein to his governors and retinue regarding taxes. And he called the protests of the subjects—even if directed to him—an act of corruption that would lead to whatever punishment the governor wished.

The shepherd drives the wolf away from the sheep. How would it be if the wolves were the shepherds?

A bedouin Arab, from among those in whom some pride remained, felt compelled to kill the governor, ignoring the punishment that this would bring from the rulers, saying: "Better to be eaten by the lion than the wolf."

Al-Azraqi[31] quotes Ibn al-Haj saying, "There is no difference between oppressors and beasts of prey except in external appearance. They have essentially the same qualities."

It is well known that the severity of coercive rule results in the loss of certain human qualities such as courage or resistance against evil or defense of manliness and love of the homeland and solicitude for it. Muslims from certain regions have become virtually "tax slaves." Their homeland and their country, the birthplace of their fathers and grandfathers, is for them only a place to give the dirham and the dinar in humility and humbleness. They are tied to ignominy like a donkey, to such extent that they abstain from love of homeland and home, stripped as they are of the qualities of the free.

This is among the greatest of reasons for the weakness and destruction of the Islamic kingdoms, as you will see—God willing—in the discussion of the Noble Rescript in this work. In it you learn the profundity of Imam Malik, may God be pleased with him, when he spoke of "the impermissibility of helping oppressive rulers put down those in revolt against them" because of that very oppression, as was mentioned above. (22) This is because oppression is among the causes of destruction leading to the extirpation of the species. All praise to Him who alone has absolute will. "He will not be questioned as to what He does, but they will be questioned" (Qur'an 21:23). And He is the Wise, the Informed.

It may be said that the ruler must in any case rely on ministers. If any person could dispense with them, then it would be Moses, the blessing of God and peace be upon him, who spoke to God. For God in His Majestic Book has him described as "the strong, the trustworthy" (Qur'an 28:26). In spite of this, Moses said to God, may He be praised: "Appoint for me a helper from my people, Aaron my brother. Increase my strength with him and let him share my task" (Qur'an 20:29–32). Thus, it can be argued that since rulers must rely on ministers, the subjects will not be in danger from any single fallible person. The answer to this, however, is that the ministers of despotic, coercive rulers are in fact executive ministers[32] carrying out the purposes of their rulers. They have no power to oppose him with an opposition that would lead to the sheathing of the sword of personal lusts. They are caught between the fang and the claw of the lion. He regards them as fowl being fattened for his appetite. And he views whatever wealth they have as part of his own wealth, for all of them are his creatures and clients. Their condition with him is like that of the tent peg that splits, no one mourns it. This obliges them to become slaves to his desires and instruments of his arrogant power. They will water down any advice given that might oppose his caprice. Indeed, out of considerations of security, a poor wretch may advise himself to flee the prospects of ruin and calamity that hover around them all. Even the upright go along with the ruler's desires, prettying up the advice given and the way it is presented.

A minister to one of the Abbasid rulers once said, "O Commander of the Faithful, if I were to advise you I would fear for myself, and if I were to keep quiet I would fear for you. My fear for you exceeds my fear of you, because you are dearer to me than I am to myself."

Whoever directs blame or criticism toward these ministers wrongs them, as God is our Witness, for one cannot be blamed who finds himself in the snare of calamity just because of a suspicion or vicious gossip, both presented without proof or demonstration, as you will see, God willing, in the second part of this volume.

The histories of Islam are laden with such stories, to such extent that the masses in the Maghrib say, "The end of everything is obscure except that pertaining to government [makhzan],[33] which is always known," meaning that it is bad. And this is because of the many examples they have seen of such. In their customary usage what they mean by "government" is "service to rulers."

(23) This fear becomes greater if the regime becomes firmly established with no challenger, and security against those who might revolt is established. Abu Muslim, the Khorasani, the great protagonist of the Abbasid revolution, said, "The most fearful of times for ministers and princes is when the populace is quiet." For this reason there are always among the ministers and princes those who would not stop looking for ways to provoke war and disorder as a means of guarding his position. It is clear that they are in a predicament of fear, and no confidence can be placed in the opinion of the fearful. He does not point out the good for its own sake. This is because the opinion of the adviser must be trusted, but if he is fearful he can not be trustworthy.

For this reason wise Europeans have said "opinion is free." This is one of their well-established maxims and rules. And in this manner also is revealed what Ibn Khaldun has reported in his *Muqaddima* in the chapter "Commercial Activity on the part of the ruler is harmful to his subjects and ruinous to the tax revenue," which reads as follows[34]:

...the Persians made no one king except members of the royal house. Further, they chose him from among those members of the royal house who possessed virtue, religion, education, liberality, bravery, and nobility. Then, they stipulated in addition that he should be just. Also, he was not to take a craft, as this would harm his neighbors. He was not to engage in trade, as he would wish to raise the prices of goods. And he was not to use slaves as servants, since they would not give good and beneficial advice.

Thus ends what Ibn Khaldun related.

It is no secret that slavery in itself does not impair human nature and does not obliterate the qualities of perfection, virtue, and religion. Slavery is a misfortune that befalls one whose original state was freedom. It does not lead to the disappearance of whatever had been shaped in him of either inherited or acquired knowledge and self-assertion, for all people are from the same clay and descendants from one man. The Prophet, may God bless him and grant him peace, said, "God removed from you the arrogance of the time of ignorance [*jahiliyya*] with its pride in ancestors. You are all from Adam and Adam is from clay. The Arab has no distinction over the foreigner except in God-fearingness. The most noble among you [in God's sight] is the most God-fearing."

Yet, the secret in the Persian stipulation is that the slave in the captivity of his master is not secure from his haughtiness, and he will call attention only to what accords with the caprice of his master. He will not call attention to the good for its own sake, nor to the interest for its own sake. He will divert his gaze from the desires of his master. Slavery in itself (24) does not lead to the lack of the good or the sound. Many notables from among the companions of the Prophet, the Followers and those who came after were former slaves unequalled in distinction, such as Suhayb al-Rumi, about whom the Messenger of God, may God bless him and grant him peace, said: "What an excellent slave is Suhayb! Even if he did not fear God he would not disobey Him." And ʿUmar ibn al-Khattab put him forward as the imam of the Muslims during the time of the consultation[35] to choose ʿUmar's successor until a new caliph could be agreed upon. And Salman the Persian, about whom ʿAli ibn Abi Talib said: "He has knowledge of the first and the last. He is a sea that is not emptied. He is one of us, the People of the House [*ahl al-bayt*]." And such as Bilal and ᶜAmmar ibn Yasir and Salim the client of Abi Hadhifa, about whom ᶜUmar ibn al-Khattab said, "If he were alive I would choose no one else than him for the caliphate of the Muslims." And Qanbar, the client of ᶜAli ibn Abi Talib and head of his police (*shurta*). And Muhammad ibn Sirin and al-Hasan ibn Abd al-Hasan al-Basri and ᶜAta' ibn Abi Rabah and Mujahid and Saᶜid ibn Jubayr, whose prayers to God were answered. When al-Hajjaj, who sought to kill him, asked, "Is it not said that your prayers are answered?" Ibn Jubayr replied, "That is what they claim." Al-Hajjaj then retorted, "Then, pray!" And Ibn Jubayr cried, "By God, may you not prevail over anyone after me." God answered his prayer, for al-Hajjaj died immediately thereafter. Al-Hajjaj in the agony of death cried, "O with me and with Ibn Jubayr." And Sulayman ibn Yasar. And Zayd ibn Aslam and Muhammad ibn al-Munkadir and Nafiᶜ, the client of Abi Nujayh and Rabiᶜat al-Raᶜi and Ibn Abi al-Zinad and ᶜAta' ibn Abdullah al-Khoransai and Makhul.

Taqi al-Din al-Maqrizi, in his book *al-Khitat*,[36] wrote in discussing the different legal schools of Islam: "ᶜUmar ibn ᶜAbd al-ᶜAziz, may God be pleased with him, gave three men the positions of mufti in Egypt. Two of them—Yazid ibn Abi Habib and ᶜAbd Allah ibn Abi Jaᶜfar—were from among the clients and one, Jaᶜfar ibn Rabiᶜa, an Arab. The Arabs disputed this, but ᶜUmar responded, 'What is my sin if the clients raise themselves by their own efforts and you do not?'"

There are other such persons who watched over the affairs of religion for the community, were molded with the characteristics of perfection, are remembered for their great works, for their courage, were in the forefront of knowledge and politics, and adorned public positions and posts of leadership. They are of such great number as not to be counted even to this very age in the Mashriq and the Maghrib. Whoever studies the *ᶜIqd al-Farid* of Ibn ᶜAbd Rabbih in his chapter on "Equality" or the *Muqaddima* of Ibn Khaldun in his chapter on "The Sciences" will see the expanded discussion of what we have referred to here.

One might well say that ministers of this kind of ruler are worse off than slaves in their slavery, because lurking behind them are the haughtiness of rulers and the slanders of the envious. (25) It is related that the vizier Jaᶜfar ibn Yahya al-Barmaki needed to give legal testimony, so he wrote his testimony and sent it to the qadi Abu Yusuf, the disciple of the great imam Abu Hanifa. The qadi, however, wrote on it a notation of rejection. This action disturbed the vizier, who went directly from his office to the palace of Harun al-Rashid and related the matter to him. Harun, infuriated, commanded that the qadi be brought before him and then asked him, "By what objection did your reject the testimony of my vizier?" The qadi replied, "I have heard him say many times, 'I am the slave of the Commander of the Faithful.' Now, if he speaks the truth, then a slave, as long as he remains in his condition of slavery, cannot have his testimony accepted, since he has to devote all of his time to the service of his master. If he is a liar, then he is to be considered unacceptable because of his lying." The vizier suddenly exclaimed, "I am the slave of the Commander of the Faithful and the qadi is in the right to reject my testimony." The vizier's later fate, however, was execution and evil consequences for him and his family. They were overthrown, and all traces of their days in power passed on to others. This was the famous Barmakid incident[37] that has been singled out for so much commentary. People have different opinions concerning the reason for the Barmakids' fall, but if persons such as the Barmakids had committed a notable crime leading to what happened to them it would not be so hidden from the most knowledgeable historians that they would differ on the matter.

The reason is simply rule according to the absolute wish of the ruler, who is not to be questioned except in the world to come where all the opposing parties meet God. Whoever leafs through the pages of histories will see what lessons are to be learned concerning such viziers.

This category—that is, the coercive absolute ruler—has disappeared, by God's grace, from most of the kingdoms of Islam, as far as we know. A certain trace of this does remain in the noble Hasani and Alawi sultanate in Fez and Marrakesh. There the sultan exercises his independent judgment in administration and the levying of taxes. He also decides what punishment is meted out to those who have committed crimes, on a fixed day of each week in a place called the *Mishwar* (place of consultation) at which the sultan appears dressed as if for war and military mobilization. That day the ʿulama' are available in a designated place for consultation if the sultan is undecided on a matter. Other cases such as retaliatory punishments (*al-qassas*), the canonical punishments (*hudud,* singular *hadd*), and all cases of human relations governed by the Religious

Law (*mu^camalat*) are judged only by the qadis, and behind them is the supervision of the ^culama'. Behind all is the supervision of the sultan.

The situation of the sultanate regarding the oath of allegiance (*bay^ca*) is that of the canonical imamate. That is, when the sultan succeeds to the throne, those possessing the power of loosening and binding, the ^culama' and sharifs, the army leaders and the notables of Fez, gather at the tomb of Mawla Idris ibn Idris ibn Abdullah ibn al-Hasan ibn Husayn ibn the Commander of the Faithful, ^cAli ibn Abi Talib, may God be pleased with all of them. The *bay^ca* sets out in writing the conditions contracted between them and the sultan on matters that fulfill the requirements of their general interest. In accepting that *bay^ca* the sultan attests before those assembled to his obligation to act in accordance with it. (26) He places his seal on that written statement while the notaries (*al-^cadul*) witness the sultan's accepting his obligation. He then swears before God to so act. At this, those assembled raise their voices, appealing to God to grant him success. This is what they regard as the true *bay^ca* between ruler and ruled. Without it there is no contractual agreement. That written agreement remains in a special place in the tomb of Mulay Idris.

If the sultan breaks his promise, the people then assemble at the tomb of Mulay Idris, and this meeting is a precursor to removing him from the throne. If the sultan returns to his commitment, the people return to their obedience. If not, they announce his dethronement and the acceptance of someone else. No one from among his retinue defends him, because the benefit of the above mentioned conditions are acceptable to all the people of the kingdom from all different classes. They see that the sultan has proceeded to break his oath, and the breaking of an oath violates justice (*^cadala*) and the position of kingship and nobility. The good is good in itself, but among those of the House of the Prophet it is even better. The bad is bad in itself, but among those of the House of the Prophet it is even more vile. The people also believe that such a sultan has broken the honor of Mulay Idris, in whose sanctuary that document was deposited.

All Morocco accepts the divine power (*kirama*) possessed by that sayyid, alive or dead. Indeed, the masses believe that the true sultan of Morocco is Mulay Idris. This accords with their goodness and Islamic simplicity in granting high honor to sharifs, ^culama', and those who do good works. It is also because of their belief and their being shaped by the Religious Law and their stopping at the limits it imposes.

This is the most important cause of their backwardness in regard to the civilization of the present time. They know this and are content with this, pleased to be among those who are not harmed by those who differ from them, awaiting God's command.

This noble sultanate, given such a situation, has set a limit at which it stops, out of consideration for that written agreement concerning the status of the rulers. Most of them are to be praised for their godliness, their following God, their implementing God's Religious Law, and their responsiveness to religious counsel. Nor is their house lacking in useful religious knowledge. Indeed, Mulay Sulayman ibn Muhammad[38] is mentioned by all for his rule. Tyrants fear his summons, the news of which is widespread. I have heard this from the notable scholar and eminent author, Abi ʿAbd Allah Muhammad al-ʿArabi al-Damnati,[39] when he passed through Tunis on his way to the Pilgrimage. I also heard stories of this sultan and his fear of God and the people's fear of his summons from our shaykh, the learned of this age and blessing of this country, Ibrahim al-Riyahi,[40] about when he visited the sultan as an ambassador sent by the Bey, Abu Muhammad Hamuda Pasha al-Husayni.[41] You will see his praise for this sultan in the biography of this shaykh, God willing. In short, the situation of such rulers resembles that of the caliphate. (27)

The findings of this lengthy but beneficial disquisition are that this category, absolute rule, is largely tyranny. Moreover, the tyranny of rulers, as has been shown, is among the strongest causes of the destruction of countries, the ruin of civilization, and the perishing of states. "And God does not harm even the weight of an ant" (Qur'an 4:40).

Thus is revealed the meaning of Ibn Khaldun's statement in the third chapter of Book One of his *Muqaddima:* "States have a natural life span, just like individuals." Ibn Khaldun sets out clear indications of this decline including the ruler's assuming all glory to himself, uprooting the group feeling with its capacity to dominate, appeals to opulence, extravagant ways, and other such things that lead to tyranny and going beyond acceptable limits.[42]

Or perhaps not, for we have seen how the Persian state and the Christian states exceeded their allotted time because the conduct of their rulers has a limit at which they stop, in accordance with politics based on reason. There is also the example of the Ottoman state, which is now in the sixth century of its existence because it observes the principles of the Religious Law and the well-regarded laws, as will be shown later, God willing.

He who makes justice his harness will have a long life. As the maxim states, "Government [*mulk*] remains in existence as long as there is justice, even if the ruler is an Ethiopian. And it does not remain with tyranny even if the ruler is an Abbasid." This is because tyranny contravenes both the Religious Law and reason (*al-Shar' wa al-ʿAql*), and whatever contravenes these two will not last. "This was God's way in the case of those who passed away of old, and you will not find any change in God's way" (Qur'an 33:62). Non-Muslims sometimes even reject the very office of monarchy.

If God should take the possessor of monarchy, then after a certain period of time the subjects may see no need for this monarchy. They thereby escape both the title and the bearer of the title. They then agree that the restraining force will be republican rule.

CHAPTER FOUR

———◆◆◆———

Republican Rule

(28) This is like the country of America and others. The essence of this category of rule is that the people choose someone to administer their political affairs and their interests for a fixed period. When that period is completed they choose another to succeed him, and so on. People may think highly of the conduct of one such individual and ask him to increase his tenure. They do not grant the one advanced to office anything of the pomp of rule or its outward signs. Rather, he is like one of them, and he carries out the decisions reached by those who are to be consulted (*ahl al-Mashwara*). They have laws that they respect with the respect Muslims accord their Religious Law, and they remain within these limits.

This category of rule has worldly benefits for the masses and the elites in that "their affairs are a matter of mutual consultation" (Qur'an 42:38). The customs of the Islamic community, however, do not provide for this category of rule, because the office of the imamate is a duty incumbent on the umma, according to the Religious Law. Those who abandon it sin, just as is the case with abandoning the duty of changing the evil, as was discussed earlier. There are Religious Laws concerning duties owed to God (*Ibadat*) and other such rulings that are based on the existence of that office, all well known in the religious books.

A noble *hadith* states, "He who dies without allegiance [*bay'a*] to an imam dies the death of the period of ignorance [*jahiliyya*]." Accordingly, the companions of the Prophet, may God be pleased with them, unanimously agreed to give priority to appointing an imam and pledging allegiance to him over burying the body of the Selected One (Muhammad), may God bless him and grant him peace. For this reason, the ʿulama' discuss the imamate in the books of the religious creeds immediately following the discussion of prophecy, emphasizing thereby its obligatory nature. The imamate is numbered among the branches, not the roots,[1] of Islamic jurisprudence (*fiqh*), according to the creeds of the religion. As the author of *al-Jawhara* (Essence of Unity)[2] has said, "The King of kings, may He be praised, created the caliph before creating his subjects." This indicates the ruler's autocracy.

(29) ʿAli ibn Abi Talib, May God be pleased with him, has said: "There are two mighty matters, one of which is properly carried out only by an individual and the other only by a group. They are kingship and correct opinion. Just as kingship is not properly secured when shared by a group, so too correct judgment is not reached by one person acting alone."

Absolute rulers took from ʿAli's words "acting alone" and interpreted them in a way that belongs only to God, who alone has absolute volition. They put aside consultation in coming to a decision, to such extent that many European notables believe that the ruler's acting alone in reaching a decision is in accordance with the Islamic Religious Law, whereas group participation in reaching a decision is republican rule. They gave the Tunisian state the name "al-Rebublikiya," meaning it had republican rule. The reason for this is as follows:

When Ottoman Sultan Selim conquered with his sword this state by means of his distinguished vizier, Sinan Pasha, may God have mercy on them, in the year 981 (1573) he left to look after Tunisia four thousand of his soldiers, of whom the leaders were the aghas, the pasha, the deys, the *bulukbashis*, and the *qadi al-ʿaskar*. The notables from among them used to meet with the notables of the country on fixed days to act on whatever matters of general interest were brought before them. When one of the French commanders saw this consultative meeting he described Tunisia's system of government as "republican rule" (*mulk jumhuri*) in the agreement signed in July 1729 (Dhu al-Hijja 1141). This agreement as amended exists in the archives of the rulers of this country. It may well be that copies can also be found with the French traders.

The fact, however, is that Tunisia is a monarchical state (*dawlat mulk*). It has never had republican rule in the Islamic period. Tunisia submitted to the authority of the Umayyads in the Mashriq and thereafter to the Abbassids, until the Sharifian Fatimids, the Banu ⁽Ubayd, became independent and challenged the Abbasid authority. The Fatimids then moved their state (*dawla*) to Egypt, and their agents in Tunisia, the Sanhaja, become independent of them.

When the rule of the Sanhaja weakened and their tyranny strengthened, Abd al-Mu'min, the second ruler of the Almohade dynasty of Berbers in Morocco, defeated them, uprooted them, and scattered them in all directions. Tunisia submitted to him, and thereafter to a number of his descendants who ruled in Morocco.

Then the Hafsids attained independence in Tunisia. They assumed the title of caliph with its many honorifics, sermons were said in their name from the pulpits of the two great mosques in Mecca and Madina[3] and their rulership expanded. Thereafter, when their nature became corrupted and their time completed, their condition deteriorated, and their end was the plundering of prosperity.

(30) Some of the dregs of the last Hafsids sought help from the Spaniards, and their soldiers alighted on this land of Islam, where they wreaked havoc. They mistreated Tunisia's holy books and her Zitouna mosque and divided up the country as the conqueror divides the conquered.

This continued until the authority of Islam in Tunisia was saved by Sultan Selim II, the son of Sultan Sulayman the Lawgiver,[4] the son of Sultan Selim, the son of Sultan Bayazid al-Wali, the son of Sultan Muhammad the Conqueror, the son of Sultan Murad, the son of Sultan Muhammad, the son of Sultan Yaldarim Bayazid, the son of Sultan Murad, the son of Sultan Orhan, the son of Sultan ⁽Uthman, from whom the name of the Ottoman dynasty is derived. Selim's soldiers proved themselves in delivering Tunisia, and this feat is reckoned among his greatest conquests. This was in 981 (1573). Tunisia thereafter submitted to him and to his successors. The sermons from the pulpits were in their name, and the names of the sultans were struck on the dinars and dirhams. This became the custom that has continued until our day. Tunisia's rulers were permitted freedom of action in accordance with the public interest (*maslaha*) as a delegation of authority from the lofty Ottoman state, sanctioned by Religious Law, because of Tunisia's distance from the

Sultanic House and the nonexistence of steamships in that day. Tunisia's rulers were also given permission to conduct jihad to bring other people into the Muhammadan religion.[5] They had other such fruits of that delegated authority. Tunisia's revenues were used for her own public interests, and her rulers would send some part of the revenue to the Ottoman state according to their ability. This was a way for Tunisia's rulers to demonstrate their obedience. This was called a "gift" to avoid using the term "payment," (al-'ada') which most Tunisians considered to have the sense of tribute (jizya).

Tunisia's governors ruled with the agreement of the people, and the Ottoman state would graciously approve their choice because this did not contradict the status of obedience. This stemmed from a desire to bring together the world of the Muslims and to close the door leading to disorders in the umma, the details of which you will see, God Most High willing, in the second part of the Muqaddima[6] to this book.

To summarize some of this, when Muhammad Bey al-Muradi exiled his uncle, Muhammad al-Hafsi, the latter went to Constantinople[7] during the time of Sultan Muhammad, who appointed him Pasha of Tunis and prepared for him an expedition of a fleet and soldiers in 1087 (1676). The opinion, however, of the people of Tunis assembled in the Great Mosque of Zitouna, was unanimous in not accepting him because of their hatred for him and their love for his nephew. When he arrived, they prevented him from landing and made known to him their intention to make war against him. Therefore, he returned. They then wrote to the Lofty Ottoman State explaining their actions as stemming from his unacceptable conduct.

A similar incident happened between Husayn ibn ʿAli Bey and Muhammad ibn Mustafa, known as Ibn Futayma. He was from among the officials of Ibrahim al-Sharif's regime, and he fled to Islambul after that regime ended, seeking refuge (31) with the Capitan Pasha. Ibn Futayma made pledges to him and reported that his effort to gain the rule in Tunisia was at the request of the people there who were awaiting him. The Capitan Pasha carried him with his fleet and landed him at Porto Farina (Ghar al-Milh). The opinion of the notables (al-mala) was unanimous against accepting him, and they made known to him their intention to resist him as well, so he returned. This was in 1127 (1715).

This was similar to the bey Hamuda Pasha's expelling ʿAli Barghal from Tripoli after having driven his deputy from Jerba, which the latter had conquered, claiming to have a *firman* from the Sultan. This was in 1209 (1794) in the reign of Selim III.

After that Hamuda sent his famous vizier, Yusuf Sahib al-Tabiʿ, to the Lofty Ottoman State to apologize, and the state accepted his apology, because in this way he had excised disorder from Islam, and the action was not seen as resisting obedience, as was actually the case. Other such incidents could be cited, all of which indicate that this province (*iyala*) is a government of monarchical rule, one of several such Ottoman provinces granted this status for reason of its geographical position. It is not a republican polity. The ruler of Tunisia, however, does have absolute authority by virtue of the Sultanic delegation. His situation differs according to the different nature of the several rulers.

Thus, Tunisia's circumstances continued to deteriorate at times and even to come to a standstill at other times until there appeared on Tunisia's horizon the first shimmerings of a constitutional dawn on Wednesday 14 Shallal 1277 (25 April 1861), and that is government limited by law.

CHAPTER FIVE

Government Limited by Law (*Qanun*)

(32) This—after the caliphate—is the rule that shields the entire community and by which corruption is removed and on which the achievement of goals depends. The possessor of this type of rule is the shadow of God on earth, to whom the oppressed appeal and who heals wounds with his justice. This is because his rule is encircled by both reason and the Religious Law. The possessor of such authority conducts himself in all his acts according to a well-known and reasonable rule that he never oversteps. He binds himself to thus act at the time of the oath of allegiance (*bay*ᶜ*a*), and he takes this oath before witnesses. If he acts so as to violate that oath, then the agreement to obey him slips from the necks of the people. It is very much like what was mentioned earlier concerning the *bay*ᶜ*a* granted the Sharifian ruler of Morocco. "And the wise stand by their commitments."[1] This is comparable to the speeches of the rightly guided caliphs upon assuming office.

The first appearance of this type of rule after the Persians was among certain people of the Christian nation. This is because the religion of the Messiah, Jesus the son of Mary, may God bless him and grant him peace, is limited to worship and coming close to God by asceticism in this world and attention to the world to come. Christian authority is over the souls, not the bodies. This left to the worldly rulers concern for this-worldly interests. Accordingly, the law at times will be in response to the demands of the subjects, producing warfare in which rivers of blood flow, as has taken place in France. The French people's sense of cohesion, fanatical zeal, and love of freedom is so mixed with their blood that they go to uncalled-for lengths. They haughtily reject the oppression of kings, as has been seen in the Frankish regions and elsewhere. The sly fox of the Arabs, ʿAmru ibn al-ʿAs, may God be pleased with him, so characterized them when he heard the noble *hadith* of the Prophet that Muslim related in the last parts of his *Sahih,* placing it in the chapter "When the hour comes, the *Rum* will be the most numerous of people."

(33) The text of the *hadith* is:

Al-Mustawrid al-Qurashi[2] said in the presence of ʿAmru ibn al-ʿAs: "I heard the Prophet of God, may God bless him and grant him peace, say, 'When the last hour comes the Byzantines [*Rum*] will be the most numerous of people.'" ʿAmr said to him, "Be careful what you say." Mustawrid replied, "I relate what I heard from the Prophet of God, may God bless him and grant him peace." ʿAmr then said, "Since you have said that, they have four attributes: they are the most forbearing of people in the face of disorder, the quickest to recover after a disaster, the readiest to regroup after flight, and the best to the unfortunate, the orphan and the weak. Their fifth good trait is that they are the most resistant to the tyranny of kings."[3]

The qadi ʿIyad has said, "The veracity of that *hadith* is demonstrated in the Christians' great numbers throughout the world and the expansion of the Christian religion such as not to be contained in a single nation [*umma*]."

There is no doubt that the fruit of oppression is destruction and the fruit of justice is prosperity, which brings increase in the masses, as indicated in the noble *hadith.* In their rejection of oppression and their benevolence to the unfortunate, the orphan, and the weak, they combat anyone who would oppress them or enslave them. They deem sweet even the taste of death until they have gained freedom and justice based on a well-established, strong, and well-known foundation respected—even by the young—with a respect given Prophetic Laws. They do not neglect the least thing in this regard, even to this day.

I heard from our friend, the wise and distinguished vizier, Khayr al-Din, who spent a long time in Paris on beylical service, the following:

I conferred with one of their notables who suddenly began to praise their ruler of that time, Napoleon III. He went on to say that he is one of those rulers who are restricted by their nature and their intelligence from doing anything other than what serves the general interest and that in this regard none of his ministers are his equal. I then asked him, "Since he reaches that degree of excellence why are you so niggardly with him in granting him powers that would not harm the constitution?" He replied smiling, "Yes, he has this characteristic, but can anyone guarantee that he will always possess this precious trait or that his son will be like him in this regard?"[4]

At times, because of the good conduct of certain rulers who are characterized by justice and love of the homeland and who compete in this world for praiseworthy traits, the constitution will be a staircase to glory and a cause of praise from the nations. It is related that one such ruler created a constitution for his subjects, and his wife criticized him saying, "You have made the position of ruler more straitened for your children than it was when inherited by you." He replied, "It is not as you think. I leave them a (34) monarchy stronger and more complete than that which I took from my ancestors." I read this account in a discerning book that one of the distinguished men of Egypt translated into Arabic from the French entitled *Qala°id al-Mufakhir fi Gharib °Awa'id al-Awa°il wa al-Awakhir* (The Proud Necklace of Unusual Customs of those from Early Times and Late).[5] He published it in one of Egypt's publishing houses that has produced excellent fruits and radiated its lights in this age.

The constitution is linked to what the times or the political situation require, as in these times when eyes and ears are open and aversion to injustice is natural. Everything can be overturned except nature, and people resemble their times more than their ancestors. He who tries to outrun the age will stumble and fall.

You surely know that the constitution of the Islamic government (*mulk*) is the majestic Qur'an and the sayings of the Messenger, may God bless him and grant him peace. God Most High has said, "We have revealed to you the Remembrance that you can show the people what has been revealed for them" (Qur'an 16:44). The Almighty has also said, "We have left nothing out of the Book" (Qur'an 6:38). Then there is what the prominent *mujtahids*, who are the heirs of the prophets, have derived from the Book (Qur'an) and the Sunna by use of analogy and upholding the purposes of the Religious Law concerning mankind. This is because the Religious Law came to extract man from the exigencies of his caprice in all circumstances both regarding worship of God and actions among men, even in governance, which is necessary to human society. It sets out the justice, mercy, faith, and the following of the public interest that is required of the ruler—even if it should go against his own desires, for he is isolated from others. He must consult concerning affairs and be led by God's command to heed the voice of those who command the good and forbid the evil and do other such things as are written in the books of the religion in order that rule may be protected according to the Religious Law. "For whosoever God has not made a light has no light" (Qur'an 24:40). And God has promised the obedient and warned the rebellious: "Whosoever does even a particle of good will see it. And whosoever does even a particle of evil will see it" (Qur'an 99:7–8).

The holder of this office will at times be desirous of God's promise and fearful of God's admonitions, such as the four rightly guided caliphs and those rulers who followed their path. From such as these come only good, for they do not transgress the constitution of the Qur'an and the Sunna. Such as these love to seek and receive advice. Power does not cause them to sin, fearing as they do that they might be as those about whom the Messenger, may God bless him and grant him peace, said: "There will be rulers (35) after me who will speak and not be answered. They will be clustered together in the fire like monkeys." This was related by Mu'awiya and transmitted by Kamal al-Din al-Damiri in Chapter Qaf of his *Hayat al-Hayawan* (Book of Animals)[6].

The people used to call to account the rightly guided caliphs and the rulers from the pulpits until the Abbasid Abu Ja'far al-Mansur forbade that. They were afraid of being called to account concerning changing what was evil. The first of the Abbasids endured considerable severity in this as in recorded in the chapter "Commanding the Good and Forbidding the Evil" in *Ihya 'Ulum al-Din* (The Resurrection of the Religious Sciences) of al-Ghazali and other such sources.

Thereafter the freedom of rulers gradually increased and their independent judgment grew, either because they received religious knowledge from certain of their 'ulama'—as was the case with the Abbasid al-Ma'mun and others possessing religious knowledge, one of the conditions of royal authority—or because of a perfection of intellect and a breadth of mental capacity so that their independent judgment resulted only in the general welfare, in most cases. Later, however, this tendency to act arbitrarily became more pronounced, the stream overflowed, and misfortune surrounded the Muslims. There appeared many among later rulers those who saw themselves as *mujtahids* within the bounds of the Religious Law without in fact having any support for this claim to *ijtihad* status other than the words "this is the way it seems to me." The truth is that such a person would see things from the perspective of individual caprice, not of rational thought, for he possessed none of the necessary instruments of *ijtihad*. Indeed, he would scarcely be able to comprehend its meaning. This would especially be the case when certain of his retinue would help him by relating stories of what rulers like him or his predecessors allegedly did in the past, or claim to see things by the light of God or other such things from among the urgings of devils and the incitement to evil ways by the flatterers of sultans. No need to inquire further about this. "And when he turns away from You he seeks to spread evil in the land and destroy the crops and the cattle. God does not love corruption" (Qur'an 2:205).

Our words apply to most of the rulers of Islam. There were, however, those among them who crossed the bridge of this world and moved on to stand before God without being vainglorious, and fulfilled promises made. "For when God's signs were read to them they would prostrate themselves" (Qur'an 19:58). "These are the party of God,[7] and it is the party of God that will prosper" (Qur'an 58:22). Such an example was the pride of the Ottoman sultans, the conqueror of countries and cities, the advocate of the truth (*haqq*) while others failed in their duty, Sultan Sulayman Khan ibn Sultan Selim Khan. For when he saw that the domination of rulers did not stop at any limit and that circumstances were leading to the weakening of Islam, the dispersal of the umma, and the disappearance of authority, he preserved it to the extent that he could in the first years of the tenth century of the Hijra, as the author Abu ʿAbd Allah Husayn Khuja has related in his history entitled *Basha'ir Ahl al-Imam bi Futuhat ʿal-ʿUthman* (The Tidings of the People of Faith Concerning the Ottoman Conquests) in a chapter that he devoted at the end of the book to the laws of the Ottoman state.

(36) Here is an abridgement of the text:

From among the laws that Sultan Sulayman ibn Selim put together and his precedent-setting acts is that one day he gathered together his courtiers from among the ʿulama', viziers, and notables, those qualified to give opinions and make arrangements, saying to them:

"All praise to the Eternal and Everlasting, whose kingdom will never disappear. Here we have followed the path of our fathers and grandfathers and we do not know what will be after us. Perhaps our descendants will include those who are virtuous and those who are wicked, those upright and others not upright. The one who turns away from uprightness may be the cause of the disappearance of this kingdom after its having been organized and cause the scattering of Islam. I have thus resolved to enact a constitution that will be able to frighten and prevent any of my descendants who might depart from the straight path in these matters.

"If any one of them should violate the Religious Law or the constitution, or neglect the duty of jihad, inclining toward leisure and neglecting the kingdom, or follow his lust or act out of personal interest, if anything of this sort should be found, what would prevent them or restrain them from so acting?"

All those in his presence gave him an answer. Then he set for them a time period to consider the matter. He then summoned them when that period had lapsed, and he listened to the answer of each. He deemed some of the answers to be good, others he put aside. Then he said, "I have seen that the soundest and most proper action is for me to place the matter in the hands of the ʿulama', who are in charge of making judgments. If they should see from any of the rulers a deficiency or fault in any aspect of these matters that have been mentioned or what is similar to them they will prevent them and restrain them for transgression, citing the text from the noble Religious Law or the constitution. The ʿulama', however, have only the resistance to be found in texts of the Book (Qur'an) and the Sunna. If the rulers do not obey their words then I charge you, in fear of Almighty God and in accordance with what came from the noble Messenger: Whosoever from among my descendants transgresses and is not deterred by the words of the ʿulama', then I place the matter in the hands of the Janissary Corps."

He then summoned the agha of the Janissaries and entrusted him with this mandate: "The admonition must come first from the

ʿulama', but if their counsel is not obeyed they will so inform you.
Then you come forward to help the ʿulama' if they must have help.
If the transgressor then obeys, fine, but if not, then he is to be
removed and someone else from among his sons or brothers or whoever is appropriate from the lineage installed in his place." As a rule
for this he established a regular session to meet every Sunday and
Tuesday, attended by the vizier and the *qadi askars*. In the chamber
was a dome-shaped elevated place overlooking the diwan, where
the sultan would sit so he could see the people and hear what they
said. All of the notables of the session had their special place. Some
five thousand soldiers would also attend. All of the notables would
be brought to the banquet table to eat. The food for the soldiers
would be in covered copper kettles. When the arrangements were
completed the *kahiya* of the Janissaries would stand up, speak to
the soldiers, and then indicate to them with the edge of his cloak to
advance. They would then lunge up to the kettles in a single attack.
Six soldiers would circle around each kettle. Then they would eat
with pleasure. This would take place every week.

If, however, the sultan or the vizier had committed a transgression, and if the sultan or the vizier had not been constrained by the
fatwa of the ʿulama' and the ʿulama' had made this known then on
the day of the diwan, the kettles would be arranged in order for the
soldiers. The *kahiya* would come before them and indicate with the
edge of his cloak to advance, in the customary way, but every one
of the soldiers would remain in his place with bowed head. Not one
would come forward. The sultan would then ask the reason, and
they would inform him of the transgression that had taken place.
He would thus be stopped and would withdraw from his transgression. If not, then this would be the sign marking the revolt leading
to his removal.

This ends the summary of Husayn Khuja's account.

I heard from certain of the ʿulama' and judges of Islambul (Istanbul)
at the time I went there as an emissary on behalf of Husayn Bey in 1246
(1830) during the reign of Sultan Mahmud, the son of Sultan ʿAbd al-
hamid I, that Sultan Sulayman committed a transgression against the
constitution and did not heed the admonition of the ʿulama'. They then
informed the Janissaries, who acted in accordance with his constitution.
Sulayman then thanked God and turned away from his transgression.

And Sulayman repeated this behavior a second and then a third time. He explained, "I did this in order to see the emergence of this constitution from potential to actual, for there is no escaping that men must work with it. They must be trained to admonish against all transgressions." May God exalt his tomb and its holiness and may God find agreeable his pure spirit and look favorably upon it. He brought faith in consultation to both the imams and the generality of the Muslims with this good tradition. Consider how he made the matter depend first upon the ʿulamaʾ, who are active in admonishing and advising,[8] guard the umma in matters of faith, know the goals of the Religious Law for believers, and know as well the meaning of the public interests and how they can be applied given worldly realities while taking into consideration the circumstances of the times by means of the clear maxims of the Religious Law. These include resisting the aggressor, turning back the harmful, (38) and gauging the extent necessity makes an act permissible. These include also protecting the believers in matters all nations deem necessary, fixing with those in authority both the rules of Religious Law and the rules of good government (*siyasa*), and determining which matters of public interest must be obeyed and which not. This is because the true constitution in Islam is the Religious Law, as has been shown. And Sulayman, may God have mercy upon him, ordered the ʿulamaʾ to do what they should rightly do. God Most High has said: "There should be from among you a nation calling for the good, commanding the good and forbidding the evil. Such as these are the successful" (Qurʾan 3:104). This is to restrain the wrongdoer so that there will be no disorder (*fitna*) in Islam. If, however, the sultan should persist in violating the Religious Law, then there remains only the force of the army, created to protect the sanctity of the faith and the people before the might of sultanic power, for obedience on the part of the creature does not extend to resisting the Creator.

There is no doubt that the transgressor can be restrained in this manner, for man in his animal nature fears swift, perceptible punishment, and there is nothing more severe to kings than being deposed. ʿUmar ibn al-Khattab, may God be pleased with him, said, "I detest governing but would not like to be deposed." With this sultan's constitution the Ottoman state grew more powerful, its cities flourished, and its followers were strengthened.

Thereafter the constitution of Sulayman weakened, and among its weaknesses was the revolt of the Janissaries against Sultan Mahmud II, may God Most High have mercy on him, described in a book written in Turkish entitled *Usus Zafer* (The Foundations of Victory).[9] This was in 1241 (1826). God helped Mahmud against them, and the sultan destroyed them, scattering them with his famous steadfastness and courage. The Nizami[10] soldiers took their place.

Their revolt was not in accordance with the Religious Law or with the constitution. Rather, it constituted injustice and corruption. Whosoever draws the sword of rebellion is killed by it, and whosoever lights the fire of disorder is burned by it.

Sulayman's constitution remained lagging and the desires of absolutism remained in the forefront, with decline on the increase, until Sultan ʿAbd al-Majid, the son of Sultan Mahmud, may God have mercy on them both, put matters right by issuing for his subjects a public covenant (ʿahd). It was named the *Khatt al-Sharif* (Noble Rescript) because of the sultanic seal (*khatt*) on it, and its different aspects have been called the beneficial *Tanzimat*. This was on 26 Shaʿban 1255 (3 November 1839). It is said that the Noble Rescript was written by his father, and the basic principles were found among his father's effects. This covenant was read in the presence of the people in the public square of the Sultan's palace, which is called the Rose Chamber. Present at this memorable pageant (39) were the sultan, ministers, ʿulama', men of state, and notables. The ambassadors sent by the kings from countries represented at the sultanic capital were invited to the procession so they could witness what he had bound himself to do before this assembly. Thus, it would be difficult for him later to turn away from it, since it would be a violation of good faith after his having confirmed it. It would reveal an indifference to the witnesses, including envoys representing their rulers. The dignity of rulers would reject such behavior. In addition, this would be to oppose the authority of the King of kings, the Most High, may He be praised. The sultan sent this covenant to all parts of his empire.

The Noble Rescript arrived in Tunis during the reign of Ahmad Bey. It was read, as required, with majesty and respect in the presence of the people, the notables from among the ʿulama', and the leading military officers in the tower courtyard of Bardo Palace on Tuesday 7 Muharram

1256 (12 March 1840). The Tunisian reply was sent, as both the Religious Law and reason would require, stating that it had been heard and would be obeyed, but that certain of its provisions would have to be postponed. This reply was in Turkish.

Then the sultan ordered that this covenant be published in the capital in Arabic, Turkish, French, Greek, and other languages. All this was sent to the remotest places in order that it would become known to the people without regard for their religion or race as a way of preserving its application. Violating what has been heard and circulated is something that dignity, reason, and human nature would reject, especially if the issue is indisputable.

The Arabic text, taken from the Egyptian publication in which the translator follows the style of the Turkish original, reads:

> All the world knows that our lofty state [dawla] from its glorious first days was ever concerned to apply the lofty principles of the Qur'an and the sublime Shariʿa laws. Our brilliant Sultanate reached the highest degree of strength and power, prosperity of our subjects, and the flourishing of our cities and villages.
>
> But in the last 150 years the former strength and prosperity have changed into weakness and poverty because of a succession of difficulties and diverse causes, the noble Shariʿa was not obeyed nor were the beneficent regulations [qawanin] followed; consequently, the former strength and prosperity have changed into weakness and poverty.
>
> It is evident that kingdoms not governed by the Religious Laws cannot survive. Certainly, from the very first day of our succession to the throne to this day, our beneficent, royal thoughts have been devoted exclusively to the development of the provinces and the cities and the promotion of the prosperity of the people, including the poor. By striving to find necessary means, the desired results will, with the aid of God, be realized within five or ten years in view of the favorable geographical position of our lofty state, its vast lands and the aptitude and intelligence of its people. Thus, with the help of the Most High and seeking the support of our prophet, we deem it important from now on to introduce new laws, basing them on firmly constructed foundations making for good administration of the lofty state. The principles of the requisite legislation are:

- Personal security
- Protecting dignity, honor and wealth
- A regular system of assessing taxes
- A means of conscripting the requisite troops

Indeed there is nothing more precious in this world than life and honor. When man sees them endangered, he is driven to adopt any means to protect them, even if his nature and temperament do not incline to disloyalty. That inescapably harms the regime and the empire. If, on the contrary, he enjoys perfect security for himself and his honor, he will not depart from the ways of loyalty and uprightness. He will concern himself with the welfare of his state and his community.

If there is no security for property, he will not trust his state and his community, nor interest himself in the prosperity of the country, being never freed of his own troubles and worries. If, on the contrary, the individual feels complete security about his wealth and his possessions, then he will become preoccupied with his own affairs, which he will seek to expand, and there will grow in him always love of the homeland, his devotion to his state and community will increase, and his endeavors will be to that end.

As for tax assessment, every state, for the defense of its provinces, needs to maintain an army and has other expenses, which can only be covered with money obtained by taxation imposed on the subjects of that state. This above mentioned taxation must be fixed appropriately. (41) Although, thank God, our well-guarded country has already been relieved of the affliction of monopolies, the harmful practice of tax-farming, which has never yielded any fruitful results, still prevails. This amounts to handing over the financial and political affairs of a country to a single person able to do as he chooses. It can even be said that it puts the country into the grasp of force and oppression, for if the tax-farmer is not of good character he will prefer his own benefit over that of others, with all of his actions based on oppression and harm. It is therefore necessary that henceforth every subject of the provinces should be taxed according to his properties, means, and affluence and that sums in excess of that should not be taken from him. Moreover there must be fixed limits to the expenses, not to be exceeded, of our lofty state for our land and seas forces and other forces set by laws that are to be applied.

Military matters, as already pointed out, are among the most important affairs of state, and it is the inescapable duty of all the people to provide soldiers to guard and defend the homeland. The situation prevailing up to the present time, however, has, first, a lack of organization and, second, is harmful to agriculture and trade. It does not take into account the provincial population. Some provinces are expected to conscript soldiers in number above their capacity and means, others to raise fewer conscripts than could be easily done. In addition, he who is conscripted into the army stays for his lifetime, which causes lassitude and despair and deprives him of the ability to raise a family. Building on this, when it is necessary to conscript soldiers from one of the provinces it must be done according to the optimal principles and with rotation in service so that the term of service for those entering the army will be four or five years. In sum, it is not hidden that strength, development, repose, and security can be achieved only by embracing these Nizami laws and carrying them out, the basis of which are the regulations mentioned above.

Henceforth, it is obligatory that those charged with misdemeanors and crimes will have their cases carefully conducted according to rules of the Religious Law. And no one of them is to be treated with insults or put to death, openly or secretly. And no incident involving one person may prejudice another. (42) Every person may possess and dispose of his wealth and properties with complete freedom and without opposition. There shall be no interference from the grandees. Should someone commit a crime, his heirs may not be stripped of their inheritance rights by the confiscation of the wealth the criminal designated for them. This protection of ours is the right of all Muslims and others from among the communities belonging to our lofty sultanate without exception.

We have decided to grant general security and complete tranquility to all the people of our well-guarded kingdom in their lives, their honor, and their wealth. We have seen fit to increase membership in the Council of Judicial Judgments (*Majlis al-Ahkam al-ʿAdliyya*) as necessary to examine and reach agreement on all cases.

The high officials of our state will meet at times with the above-mentioned council. Every one of them will offer his advice and approval without restraint or concern in order that the requisite laws ensuring security in matters of life, wealth and tax assessment will be implemented.[11]

The discussions and negotiations concerning the military *Tanzimat* will be in the Consultative Chamber (*Dar al-Shura*) at the gate of the Commanding General's headquarters (*Siraskariyya*) and whenever a law has been formulated it will be shown to me to approve and adorn with my auspicious seal that it may become operative as God Most High wishes.

Since the Religious laws are established essentially to give life to religion and rule (*mulk*), this is a promise and compact from our regal person that there will not issue from us anything that may violate it. I swear before God in the Chamber of the Noble Cloak (*Bayt al-Kharqa al-Sharifa*)[12] in the presence of all the ʿulama' and delegates. The ʿulama' and delegates will also take this oath.

In sum, anyone, whether from the ʿulama' or the viziers, who acts in violation of these laws based on the *Shariʿa* will be subjected in accordance with this constitutional decree (*Qanunname*) to a punishment appropriate to his confirmed crime without regard for rank or concern for person.

Since all the officials have a salary, and the situation is such, and an adequate pension, and he who does not have an adequate pension will be granted what is needed, strong laws must exist to stop and prevent the despicable bribery and corruption, (43) forbidden by the Religious Law and the most powerful corrupter of states.

Inasmuch as the intent of these clear means and principles is to abrogate and change the old ways in their entirety, this sultanic decree will be presented to the ambassadors of the friendly nations residing in our lofty capital (*dar al-saʿadah*) that they may be witnesses to its permanency and applicability to the end of time, God Most High willing. It must also be distributed to the people of Istanbul and to all of our well-guarded provinces.

And whosoever acts to violate these laws established on a solid foundation, may God, the angels, and all the people damn him and may he not be saved on judgment day.

We ask God the Munificent to grant us all success in comprehensive blessing.

———◆———

The oath taken in such important matters is not to be disavowed. Al-Suyuti in his *Awwaliyat* (First Things) relates that Muʿawiya, may God be pleased with him, was the first to have the soldiers swear obedience before God Most High, and ʿAbd al-Malik ibn Marwan had them swear a solemn oath. The well-known *bayʿa* for the Abbasids took place in the judicial diwans with solemn oaths, and a procession to God's house, the giving of alms as well as other serious acts.

The oath taken involves obedience to a powerful creature, and it is intended to establish a case, forcing him to observe its terms. The oath taken in the Chamber of the Prophet's noble cloak is, however, a vow to obey God. It is a vow to show gentleness to God's creatures in accordance with the justice that is God's measuring scale in this world. God has said, "Do not break your oaths after having affirmed them, for you have made God your Guarantor. God knows what you do" (Qur'an 16:91).

These fundamentals prevail now in the Sublime Ottoman State. By them undeniable progress and prosperity have come to the Ottoman State of Islam, and the Sultan Sulayman of this age, Sultan ʿAbd al-Aziz, has strengthened and institutionalized them. From the time he sat upon the throne he has awakened his sagacity and put to sleep his passions. He has replaced extravagant in opulence with factors making for prosperity and the requirements for nobility. He has been a faithful trustee (44) of God's wealth and that of His creatures. He has risen above the outward signs associated with his ancestors such as being adorned in jewels during celebrations. He has caused distant hope to come near and has cancelled unnecessary projects. He has virtually limited expenses to what is essential and useful and what requires immediate attention. He is graciously disposed to use the wealth entrusted to him for the common good. He works to increase what will enhance utility for the country and does other such things that are made known in the newspapers in many different places and languages. His deeds are on the lips of those who arrive from the Ottoman capital. God has provided him with such individuals as ministers of whom it can be said "When God wishes the best for an imam He sends him a righteous minister who reminds him when he forgets and helps him when he remembers." This tradition of the Prophet is given credence in our times by the notables of the Sublime State, such as the famous minister of lofty reputation throughout the inhabited world, Fu'ad Pasha,[13] and those who, like him, are molded in the highest morality. They direct their concerns to the public interest and to giving advice for the sake of their faith, their sultan, and their country. We ask God to further the condition of this umma and to use these ministers to brighten the blackest darkness.

I say that it does not escape the thoughtful, just, and believing person, one whose religion is "advice belongs to God and to His Messenger and the imams of the Muslims and the generality of the people" and whose faith is "love of the homeland," that constitutional government is required by both the Religious Law and reason. Only in this way can there be probity for the umma in this age, as has been said in the Noble Rescript. In sum, strength, prosperity, repose, and security can be attained only by the well-ordered laws.

The ruler of such a dominion is loved and obeyed. In his hand is the power protecting the religion and the kingdom. After the assemblies have decided on the laws, they are not implemented unless he so rules by signing them. It is he who selects those whom he, with the light of his reason, deems qualified for the various religious (*Shar'iyya*) and political (*siyasiyya*) offices. They are his deputies. It is he who declares peace and war. He designates his successor, because he is the trustee relating to his subjects like the father to his children. He commands the army, which may not embark on legally sanctioned warfare (*qital shar'i*) without his permission. It is under his aegis that those responsible for carrying out religiously mandated collective duties (*furud al-kifaya*) are appointed. He is the guardian for those Muslims who have no guardian. Other such characteristics of this office, based on reason and tradition, could be mentioned.

Both religious (*Shar'i*) and political (*siyasi*) laws mandate that the subjects obey him. They must honor the rights due him. They should love him, glorify him, and assist him. They should defend him against those who wrongly rebel against him. They should pray for him and advise him. As the proverb asserts, "Esteem based on fear is transitory, esteem based on justice is ever increasing."

(45) The laws of this category of government vary according to the different peoples, geographical conditions, time periods, and customs. For all, however, justice is the mainspring. It is well known that justice is a necessity. These different laws are the means to that end. Considerations of the end influence the means.

The details of the law are either based on explicit Religious legal texts (Shar‘i) or derived from the sense of the Religious Law (Sharī‘a) or are based on Siyasa Shar’iyya.[14] This latter includes the actions which, even if not set out in the Religious Law or those that are an inspiration brought down from heaven, bring people closer to righteousness and farther from corruption. For God has sent messengers in order that the interests of His creatures be realized. Whenever we find a public interest not categorically in conflict with a text and we assume it is required by the Religious Law, then it should be authorized because the rulings of the Religious Law are intended to protect its goals concerning mankind. And what greater goals are there than justice and the means to attain it?

‘Umar ibn ‘Abd al-‘Aziz, may God be pleased with him, said, "People will face as many legal sentences as the iniquity they cause." ‘Izz al-Din ibn ‘Abd al-Salam added, "And as many judgments in the fields of administration [siyasat], transactions [mu’amalat], and precautionary acts [ihtiyatat] as their acts provoke." Shaykh al-Fasi related this in his commentary on the Lamiyyat al-Zaqqaq (al-Zaqqaq's Lamiyyat). Al-Azraqi,[15] in his book Bada’ia’ al-Silk fi Taba’i al-Mulk (The Marvels of Conduct in the Characteristics of Rule) in commenting on al-Tartushi said: "The infidel sultan who guarantees correct policy is more durable and stronger than a just, believing sultan who is neglectful of rule according to the religiously based regulations [siyasa shar‘iyya]. Well-ordered oppression is more durable than neglectful justice, for there is nothing more suitable to a sultan than effectively ordering affairs and nothing more corrupt than neglecting them. A sultan, whether a believer or an infidel, will prevail only with strong justice or good organization."

If you follow the details of the laws in all their variety, you will not find them violating the requirements of justice deemed necessary in every community. They close the door against injustice.

Whosoever wants to peruse a precise passage on this has only to read the third section of the third chapter of the book of the eminent and lofty Rifa‘a Rafi‘ al-Tahtawi, the Egyptian, which he wrote concerning his journey to Paris. It is called Takhlis al-Ibriz fi talkhis Bariz (Refining Gold in Epitomizing Paris).[16] There he summarizes French law in a wonderful way that bears witness to his objectivity and perceptiveness. He writes in it:

Let me mention to you that even if most of what is in French Law
is not found in the Book of God Almighty, nor in the Sunna of the
Prophet, may God bless him and grant him peace, you should know
how they reasoned that justice and impartiality (46) cause the flourishing of kingdoms and the well-being of people. The rulers and the
subjects have been so led by this that their country has increased in
population, their knowledge has grown, their wealth accumulated
and their hearts put at ease. One never hears anyone complain of
oppression. Justice is the foundation of prosperity.

We witnessed the same when we traveled to Paris with Marshal
Ahmad Bey in 1261 (1846).

The commander of commanders, the minister Khayr al-Din, concurs
in this matter in his book, *Aqwam al Masalik fi Ma'rifa Ahwal al-Mamalik*
(The Surest Path to Knowledge of the Conditions of Countries). In that
book, he gathered together pearls of politics that adorn political leadership. He translated most of these examples from French books in a
delightful and exotic rhetorical style that bears witness to the author's
attainment and strength in eloquence.

Ibn Khaldun has written in his *Muqaddima*, in the chapter entitled
"The Meaning of the Caliphate and the Imamate," the following:

> The real meaning of kingship is that it is a form of organization nec-
> essary to mankind. It requires superiority and force, which express
> the wrathfulness and animality of human nature. The decisions of
> the ruler will therefore usually deviate from what is right. They will
> be ruinous to the worldly affairs of the people under his control,
> since as a rule he forces them to execute his intentions and desires,
> which may be beyond their ability. This situation will differ accord-
> ing to the difference of intentions to be found in different genera-
> tions. It is for this reason difficult to be obedient to the ruler.
> Disobedience makes itself noticeable and leads to trouble and
> bloodshed. Therefore, it is necessary to have reference to ordained
> political norms, which are accepted by all people and to whose laws
> they submit. The Persians and other nations had such norms. The
> dynasty that does not have a policy based on such norms cannot
> fully succeed in establishing the supremacy of its rule. "This is how

God proceeded with those who have gone before"(Qur'an 33:62).
If these norms are ordained by the intelligent and leading personal-
ities and best minds of the dynasty, the result will be governance
based on reason [siyasa ʿaqliyya]. If they are ordained by God
through a lawgiver who establishes them as religious laws, the result
will be religious governance [siyasa diniyya], which will be useful
for life in both this and the other world.[17]

In his book al-Maqasid (The Aims), Shaykh Abu Ishaq al-Shatibi[18]
has written in the same vein in discussing "The Purpose of the Lawgiver
in placing the responsible human being (al-mukallaf) under the rulings
of the Religious Law (Shariʿa)," after citing Shariʿa texts condemning
human willfulness:

> And third, as is known from experience and custom, (47) worldly
> and otherworldly interests are not attained by aimlessly following
> one's whims and intentions with the accompanying struggle, strife,
> and ruin, all of which is against the attaining of such interests.
> Continuous experience and custom makes this known. Thus there
> is general agreement that the one who follows his appetites and goes
> as they lead him is blameworthy. Indeed, those with no religious
> law to follow or whose religious law has faded away must follow
> worldly interest to restrain by reason anyone acting according to his
> own willfulness, and they agree only on what seems sound to them
> and sanctioned by custom. This is what they call civil policy [siyasa
> madaniyya].

It follows that human prosperity inescapably requires a well-known
and well-kept policy by which the ruler organizes his affairs. That is realized only by either Religious Law or rational law. That is the meaning of
the above-mentioned Noble Rescript, which said, "It is evident that kingdoms not governed by the laws of the Shariʿa will not survive." And
glory to Him who said, "And if the Truth had followed their desires then
the heavens and the earth and all who were in them would have been
corrupted." (Qur'an 23:71). He is the Prime Mover, the Chooser, the
Wise, and the Experienced. "He is not to be asked what He does. They
are to be asked" (Qur'an 21:23).

It is well understood that the policy imposed by the Lawgiver in all its details became difficult when, after the end of the caliphate, kingship devolved to the well-known dynasties and to particular places, such as Muʿawiya designating his son Yazid as his successor, claiming that the circumstances of the time required that. The situation of Islam changed from the original simplicity and turning away from the luxuries of this world to civilization and immersion in finery and extravagance. In any case the community defending its territory must inescapably prepare the protective strength needed such as fortresses and ships in maritime countries and other such instruments of defense as required in all times. Soldiers must be trained to take their places in the battle lines. There are other such matters that did not exist at the beginning of Islam. The circumstances of our times have made these things necessities, for to achieve the object of such preparations and precautions is to resist harm to the extent possible. This is all taken into consideration in the Religious Law, and it is not possible without wealth that is obtained in every way. The Religiously Legal income in these times may not be adequate to these ends. For that reason absolute rulers have extended their hands to the wealth of the subjects and to their very lives should they defend their wealth. They send their entourage of hunting predators with instruments to entrap God's creatures (48) and seize without limit. This is what the Noble Rescript referred to as causing destruction.

A wise person has said, "If the hands of the provincial governors reach too far, disorder ensues in the treasuries, bringing a deficit leading to destruction." Seeing is believing. Wealth is second in importance after life itself, and avarice is the natural disposition of mankind. God Most High has said: "If you believe and are God-fearing you will receive your due. He will not demand your worldly wealth. If He should ask it of you and even press you, you would be niggardly. He would thus reveal your secret malice" (Qur'an 47:36–37).

Al-Bukhari in his *Sahih* (The True) has related from Abi Hurayra, may God be pleased with him, who heard al-Sadiq al-Masduq (the Prophet Muhammad), God's prayers upon him, say, "When God's covenant of protection [*dhimma*] and that of the Prophet, may God bless him and grant him peace, is violated then God, All-Powerful and Glorious, hardens the hearts of the people covenanted, and they hold back what they possess." His statement "God's covenant of protection and that of the Prophet is violated" means carrying out unacceptable tyranny and oppression. This *hadith* is among the most distinguished on prophecy as al-Maqrizi has said in his book *al-Khitat*.

ʿAbd Allah ibn al-Habhab, the official in charge of collecting the land tax in Egypt, wrote to Hisham ibn ʿAbd al-Malik that the land of Egypt could bear a tax increase, and he increased for each dinar a qirat. And the Egyptians revolted in the year 107 (725–26). The resulting turmoil and war continued until 216 (831–32), when the Abbasid caliph Ma'mun arrived personally and brutally deposed the governor. It was the same with the revolt in the Morea and the Greek Islands in 1236 (1821). There is no cause for this except the injustice of tax collection and the tyranny of the harsh and violent tax-collectors appointed. Stories told about them would cause the flesh to crawl. These are violations of God's covenant and that of the Prophet. As has already been related, these people were especially resistant to the oppression of rulers. Their descendants have remained so. This resistance is a very human disposition, unless bound by the restraining hand of the Religious Law.

Emphasizing the position of the covenant and jihad in Islam is necessary because many of the ignorant, who know nothing of Islam except the name, do not understand the meaning of covenant (*dhimma*)[19] or the respect it has in the Islamic community, for it imposes on us rights in favor of the *dhimmis*. According to the covenant of God and His Messenger and the religion of Islam, *dhimmis* are guests in our community and under our protection. Whosoever attacks them, even if only by a evil word, (49) assails the reputation of any one of them, or commits any harm, or abets in such acts violates the covenant of God, the Prophet, and the religion of Islam. The Prophet, may God bless him and grant him peace, has said, "I oppose whoever attacks a *dhimmi*. Whosoever in my name harms a *dhimmi* has me for an enemy." He also has said, "Concern yourselves with the lot of the *dhimmis*." And the last of what Muhammad, may God bless him and grant him peace, has said on this subject was "Protect me in my *dhimma*." There are other such noble prophetic *hadiths*.

It is the duty of every Muslim to keep the Prophet's dhimma. Ibn Hazm relates in *Muratib al-Ijma'* (The Degrees of Consensus)[20] that even if infidels (*ahl al-harb*) came to our lands seeking those under the *dhimma* it would be our obligation to go forth and fight with whatever resources available to us, even die, in protecting those under the covenant of God and His Prophet. Surrendering them without such resistance would be to neglect the covenant.

This consensus of the community imposing even loss of life or wealth in order to protect the *dhimmis* from destruction demonstrates its great importance. For God sent the messenger of this umma, the seal of the messengers, to all mankind, calling them to faith in God and each individual to submission to God and to observing the pillars of Islam. He who responded to Him became at that moment one of the Muslims, having whatever rights they have and whatever duties they have. He who refrained from doing so, after having been given notice, was to be fought, his possessions taken as lawful booty, and he enslaved. The purpose of this was that he may enter into the religion of Islam, not for a worldly purpose such as booty and the like. No value is given to such things in the view of the Lawgiver. Thus, he who fights for the sake of booty does not have the armature of a holy warrior in God's way.

The word jihad, as Ibn Rushd has said, is from the root j-h-d, which means exertion. The meaning of jihad in God's way is the utmost in tiring exertion for the sake of God, may He be praised, and to glorify the word of God that makes it the road to paradise and the way thereto. God Most High has said, "And strive for God with the effort that is His due" (Qur'an 22:78).

Jihad is comprised of four parts: jihad of the heart, jihad of the tongue, jihad of the hand, and jihad of the sword. Jihad of the heart is to strive against Satan and the struggle of the self against forbidden appetites. Jihad of the tongue is to command the good and forbid the evil. Jihad of the hand is to restrain the misdeeds and aggressions of rulers and carry out the canonical punishments as necessary. (50) Jihad of the sword is to combat against the polytheists.

Anyone who exerts himself for the sake of God Most High has conducted jihad in God's way, but the expression "jihad in God's way" refers to combating infidels with the sword in order that they will enter into Islam or pay the *jizya* as an act of submission. This is a communal obligation *(fard kifaya)*. It is related that to the imam Sahnun it is an aspect of orthodoxy *(sunna)*.

If those called to Islam choose to enter into the covenant by paying the *jizya*, Muslim rule will be imposed upon them in accordance with the conditions they have accepted. The Lawgiver, in imposing the *jizya*, is concerned with the interests of the afterlife, trusting that they or their children will embrace Islam. Thus, his *jizya* allows for them to submit as is necessary to the hand of the vanquisher with obedience and submission, the lot of the ruled with the ruler. Because humans naturally dislike this submissive state, it may guide them to the light of faith. It is thus not a matter of enslavement. Nor is the *jizya* designed that they may remain in their polytheism, for wealth is not to be derived from an act of resistance to God, and polytheism is the greatest resistance to God.

The contract of *jizya* provides a protection for life, as does converting to Islam. God imposes upon the Muslim all of his commandments in the contract (*aqd*) of his embracing Islam just as He obliges the *dhimmi* to obey all the conditions of his pact of protection in entering into the covenant. And just as rejection of the commandments of God in Islam is divided into that which invalidates the contract—making licit bloodshed and the taking of wealth—and that which does not invalidate the contract but only requires punishment and reprimand, so also are the conditions of the *jizya* contract divided into those that invalidate the pact of protection—such as warfare or resisting the orders of the sultan—and those that do not invalidate the contract. These are great acts of corruption, which call for punishment.

Anyone who wishes to study the details of all this should refer to chapter 118 of the *Furuq* of Shihab al-Din al-Qarafi.[21] In that he mentions the agreement of the four imams concerning what invalidates that contract and what does not invalidate it. Or one can consult the works on the general principles of law known as *al-Ashbah wa al-Naza'ir*[22] and the *Ahkam al-Sultaniyya* of al-Mawardi.[23] He states in the chapter "The *Jizya* Contract" that "according to Abu Hanifa, only a resort to arms invalidates the contract. Even if the *dhimmis* violate their commitments it is not permissible to kill them unless they resort to arms. They must then be safely expelled from Muslim lands so that they may find refuge. If they do not leave willingly then they are to be expelled forcibly." So one sees the concern for the *dhimma* contract in the religion of Islam.

(51) When one converts to Islam, his *jizya* status is removed and he becomes just like his fellow Muslims. This is because the purpose of the

jizya is not the taking of wealth. Only Hajjaj ibn Yusuf imposed the *jizya* on Muslim converts.

In the *Khitat* of al-Maqrizi: "The Amir of Egypt, Hayyan ibn Shurayh, wrote to ʿUmar ibn ʿAbd al-ʿAziz, may God be pleased with him, 'After salutations, truly Islam has harmed revenue (*jizya*) to such extent that I had to borrow from al-Harith ibn Thabita twenty thousand dinars to cover the payments due the members of the diwan. If the Commander of the Faithful will see fit to order me to collect the *jizya* I will do so.' ʿUmar wrote in reply, 'After salutations, your letter has reached me. I gave you the command of the Army of Egypt even though I knew your weakness. I have ordered my messenger to strike you on your head with twenty blows. To impose the *jizya* on those who convert to Islam, God denounce your suggestion! God sent Muhammad as a righteous guide, not as a tax collector. Upon my life! Yea, upon the life of the most miserable of those who caused the people, all of them, to embrace Islam at his behest.'"

Perhaps his punishment was because of his ignorance of the purposes of the Religious Law toward mankind, for the *jizya* was made to lead people to Islam, as has been shown. How could he bring harm to that? Therefore, ʿUmar corrected Shurayh in this matter, knowing his weakness, just as a father would discipline a son. This is the meaning of the covenant and *jizya* in the Islamic religion. There can be no tyranny, no oppression, no violence, no insubordination, and no easy lapsing into strife.

For this and like reasons, a constitution is absolutely necessary in order that the human lives and sacred bodies will not be prey to predatory governors and tax collectors. For the evil consequences return to the state, either through the destruction of lives and wealth as a result of their being dominated and coerced, as happened in Egypt, or by a portion of the kingdom entering into revolt, as happened in the Greek Isles. The Noble Rescript refers to that.

With the existence of the just constitution the rebel becomes a wrongdoer, repudiating God's bounty. He who denies God's bounty deserves retribution. Let us look at some of the chapters of the constitution, which provides for security of the person, wealth, and honor. These include equality among people in human rights, which includes the right to equity in judgments, there being no difference in that between the virtuous and the opposite. There is no denying the differences between the sons of Adam in characteristics and human virtues. The Most High has said, "God wishes to remove from you all uncleanness, Oh People of the household, [ahl al-bayt] and to give you a thorough cleansing" (Qur'an 33:33). And the Most High has asked, "Are those who know and those who do not know equal?" (Qur'an 39:9). (52) These differences, however, are of no consequence in affecting judgments. This is referred to in the Noble Rescript. It is not hidden that this equality is one of the bases of justice. The Commander of the Faithful, ʿAli ibn Abu Talib, may God be pleased with him and honor his face, brought a case against a Jew, and he treated his opponent as an equal before the judge. The judge hesitated to accept the charge as clearly proven, even though ʿAli was who he was, and said to him, "Your two witnesses or his oath." When the two of them left, the Jew admitted to the charge. It concerned a bow, which he returned to ʿAli. Then he embraced Islam.[24] Consider the natural disposition to love justice, how it led to a man's leaving his religion, which is more precious to him than any other value. Yet, it might have resulted in quite the opposite—God is our refuge. "Learn a lesson, you who have eyes" (Qur'an 59:2). This has been referred to in the Noble Rescript concerning protecting the person and honor, "When a man sees person and honor endangered, he is driven to adopt any means to protect them." Inequality leads to jeopardy that causes the reasonable person to try to protect himself. Proof of this is evident to the eyes. Necessity permits what is otherwise prohibited.

Accordingly, no judgment should be rendered against a person concerning himself or his wealth except following numerous warnings. And the defendant has the right to bring his case before another court in order to eliminate his straitened circumstances and be reassured. This is sound judicial policy, for the ʿulama' have said, "The judge does not pass judgment except in the presence of the legally learned [ahl al-ʿilm] and with their consultation." The imam al-Maziri has said, "The judge is obliged to consult even if he is one of the ʿulama'." This is because what those learned in jurisprudence (fuqaha, singular faqih) think about a case and what they discuss gives one a confidence that he would not otherwise have if facing a single person arbitrarily expressing his opinion. The maxim states that "He who acts arbitrarily errs and he who lords it over the people is contemptible."

Among these things is the matter of taking revenue from the subjects and spending it for their proper interests. This is the axis around which turns in all countries either the flourishing or the ruin of cities. Well-protected wealth is one of the strongest fortresses. This is what is meant by tax (*wurku, virgi* in Turkish) in the Noble Rescript. Those drafting the constitution set aside a portion of the wealth for the office of the ruler as appropriate to the country's prosperity, wealth, size, and greatness for him to spend on his personal needs. This is not to be disallowed. The companions of the Prophet, may God be pleased with them, when agreeing unanimously to offer the oath of allegiance to Abu Bakr the Righteous, may God be pleased with him, forbade him to engage in trade. They set up from the state treasury a fixed sum for him appropriate to the circumstances of the time and his asceticism. It was likewise with ʿUmar, may God be pleased with him. If the ruler takes the state revenue designated for him, the remaining wealth is for the country and the people under his stewardship. He is to spend it only for the public interest as defined by the religious law or by wise policy.

(53) Without consultation, the public interest is not realized and accepted by all the people. The Most High said to his impeccable messenger, who does not speak capriciously: "If you had been rough and hard-hearted they would have dispersed away from you. So forgive them and ask them to forgive you and consult them in the matter" (Qur'an 3:159). Hasan al-Basri has said, "Muhammad, may God bless him and grant him peace, did not need to consult them, but he wanted it to become the accepted tradition for rulers." And al-Azraqi relates from al-Tartushi: "Consultation is among the things that the wise deem to be the foundation of the kingdom and the basis of sovereign rule. Both the ruler and the ruled need it." Al-Azraqi said: "That is the way it is, letter by letter in the Religious Law." The qadi Ibn al-ʿArabi said "Consultation in at the root of religion and God's sunna for this world and the world to come. It is obligatory on all creation from the Messenger to the least person after him. Among the sayings of our master ʿAli, may God honor his face, 'Nothing is right when consultation is missing.'"

When the best thinkers compete in the field of consultation, the results of these first steps are presented to the ruler and he signs it, this becomes a decree that must be obeyed, for no one can then say "What remains of my wealth has been taken and spent without addressing the needs of my country." If wealth is taken and spent according the views of one individual who is not to be questioned, that will lead to deficiency, for that view will vary as do individual opinions and aims.

A ruler may prefer to rely on compelling royal force, seeing that as an instrument for subduing and carrying out his whims. He increases the number of soldiers and their weapons. This leads to instability. The increase is unnecessary and is not appropriate to the circumstances of the country. With heavy state expenditures, the sail becomes larger than the ship. And the expenditures of the kingdom are burdened by what must be spent on the soldiers. Revenue is lost, since the soldiers are withdrawn from productive work. There is also the lack of rational planning in the policy of conscription, for the ruler conscripts as he wishes, not as might be required of him. All this has been mentioned in the Noble Rescript.

A ruler also might rely on the majesty of the state and the splendor of kingship and the ways of greatness by building such things as lofty public buildings and castles, for which there is no need except for personal pleasure stemming from love of haughtiness, majesty, and excess. (54) He may claim that in such things is found remembrance, but not a pretty remembrance. The Umayyad caliph Nasir, the builder of al-Zuhra in al-Andalus said:

> The ambitions of rulers, if they want to be remembered, are expressed in the tongues of buildings. A building, if magnificent, bears witness to the ruler's great standing.

That hint of devastation leads to disaster in his kingdom, especially if these temples and palaces are of materials from outside the kingdom, for that is truly like one who destroys a city to build a palace.

There may be for some rulers a laudable purpose in this, like he who builds what may be required in times of famine and hunger to meet the needs of the poor and to forestall their protests and riots by providing work.

Some rulers favor hoarding and storing wealth until times of need, as they allege. They leave it idle in rooms under lock and key. They do not notice that being thus locked up it is put to no use. All works of this world revolve around the axis of the two noble coins, gold and silver.

Wealth creates wealth and men secure gains working with others. The storehouses of rulers are the hearts of their subjects. Whatever they deposit in them they will always find.

Some seek to emulate the great rulers, whose kingdoms have no need for others in all of their requirements, ignoring the circumstances of their kingdoms or the deficiencies that their emulation, lacking direction, measure, or discrimination will create. It is as happened with the petty kings (*muluk al-tawa'if*) in Spain whom Ibn Rashiiq al-Qayrawani reproached by saying:

> What spoils my pleasure in the land of Andalus are the names such as Mu^ctasim and Mu^ctadid—royal titles without kingdoms. It is like the puffed up cat declaiming with the force of the lion.

You see the likes of these who pay attention only to those above them, the very opposite of what the Messenger had ordered. Thereby they "destroy their homes with their own hands" (Qur'an 59:2), greedily absorbed in this emulation, the result being that income does not cover expenses.

(55) When they reach that condition, their kingdom lacks the basic revenue, not to mention any additional income. "He who buys what he does not need sells what he needs." Often they become indebted for other than essentials. "And indebtedness is a worry by night and a humiliation by day." What deceives them—and the passions are deceptive—is that certain European states do borrow. They do not think this through, because reason is asleep while desire is awake, and the appetite blocks out the light of understanding. These debts incurred by European states are not due to the vainglory of their kings or out of a sense of humiliation. Rather they incur loans when there is a need to finance a beneficial project deemed sound by those qualified to be consulted. This loan is raised from their own subjects, those of wealth induced to do this by the justice and reliability of the laws.

In their countries a fixed amount of interest on the money loaned is permitted, which the government never exceeds, for the holy laws according to the texts of the Torah, the Evangel, and especially the Muhammadan Religious Law (*Shari^ca*) forbid the charging of interest. They are strict in this prohibition because such gain belongs only to God, just as is the case with all booty and offerings. If one takes interest, its benefits accrue to him and not to God alone. In sum, the prohibition of interest (*riba*) in the Islamic Religious Law is a matter of worshipping God, for God forbade it in His Book and warned against it.

Non-Muslims see the reason for its prohibition in the harm done to the debtor. They are thus willing to negotiate the paying of a harmless amount of interest as a transactional necessity. In this way you find that the wealthy among them are inclined to offer with this slight interest their fully secured capital in order to be free of monitoring its growth in gainful trade that may or may not reap a profit. The profit gained from the debts of these rulers accrues to the people of these countries. It does not go abroad. This is because of their pride in the wealth of their subjects, which bears witness to the justice of the rulers. For example, the national debt in England and also in other countries is money that stays in the country and produces more income than that earned from residences and other real estate. The intelligent subjects actually prefer the notes designating these debts over gold and silver because of their lightness. If the owner of these notes needs his money in cash he will have no trouble obtaining a buyer, either at a profit to the seller or at least a satisfactory return on capital. If he is in a hurry he can obtain cash at a bank at a slight, trifling discount.

(56) Thus also with France, the governmental debts held by the people are on a par with holdings of real estate. It is related that when the present ruler of the French, Louis Napoleon III, required money for the Crimean War, in agreement with the National Assembly[25] he ordered his minister to solicit the loans in the amount needed and found within hours subscriptions exceeding several times over the amount specified. He then said to his minister: "We have no need for this excess. We will take loans only from the weak who have subscribed to small amounts" preferring that they profit from the interest to help them increase their wealth. What greater pride can the rulers of this world have than this? Their treasuries are the wealth in the hands of their subjects. They are like a father to his sons.

In any case, the holy laws, reason, and human nature show that he who is without debt is better off than the indebted, even if only to his own sons. The Messenger of God, may God bless him and grant him peace, has said, "Oh God, I seek refuge in You from indebtedness and the mastery of men." This is the case if it is without the paying of interest. If it is with interest then the matter is more difficult, both according to reason and the Religious Law (*ʿaqlan wa sharʿan*), for God warned against no disobedience more severely than that concerning interest. God Most High said, "Oh ye who believe, fear God and relinquish what remains due to you of interest if you are believers. If you do not, then beware of war from God and His Messenger" (Qur'an 2:278–279). Who has the strength to be at war with God and His Messenger? The disobedience against God in paying interest is less than that of accepting interest. Many Muslims carelessly pay interest upon necessity, or what they call necessity. For often such a person can find someone to give him a fatwa that necessity is whatever each person decides it to be.

I have been told that wise advisers to kings in Europe, both past and present, take this issue of debt very seriously. They do not enter into it lightly, but only upon fully authenticated necessity so that it would be the lesser of two evils. This is because of the disasters they know from experience to expect. Such dangers are avoidable but for individual self-indulgence and loss of self-control. The excellent ʿAli ibn Abu Talib said, "May God have mercy on the one who knows his capacity and does not exceed his limits." There are other examples concerning expenses for such purposes, closed to review or demurrer, leading to chronic sickness, brought about by the making of a loan.

If the person in charge of finances would seek counsel, which is the seed of wisdom and guide to the right way, as was set out in the Noble Rescript, he would quickly determine the public interest (57) and would give priority to the absolutely necessary over the necessary and both of these over those matters that call for improvement.

There is nothing more deleterious to development and more likely to lead to destruction than giving priority to matters needing improvement over those absolutely necessary. Proof of this is to be seen and experienced, for improvement before setting aright that which is to be improved is repugnant. It is like painting the wall of a dilapidated house before fixing its foundation. The hand of the painter would bring down what was to be painted.

Consider the situation of the Europeans (*al-Ifranj*), who have achieved such a development in their countries that one hearing about it would almost not believe until seeing for himself. Note how they approach matters with thoughtful deliberation. They establish just laws so that security is assured, they taste its sweetness and find shelter in its shade. They conduct their affairs and work to expand the circle of their livelihood and wealth. Hope is thus strengthened, work is secured, and necessity calls them to increase it. They make factories for spinning and weaving and for iron working. They work like the carpenter planing his wood and do other things that fulfill needs, and increase production with a brisk trade of buying and selling outside their countries. All this is most readily facilitated by ready interchange, easing their paths at sea with steamships and on land with secure and smooth roads, enabling carriages to reach all places. They go up the mountaintops with the same ease as in the plains. Then they create centers for exchanging the teams of animals to maintain speed. Thus many legs of a journey are accomplished in little time.

They have created a postal service to carry the letters that facilitate intercourse. And as the current of development and civilization abundantly flowed upon them they produced iron roads on which steam-powered carriages can speed. All this has caused their countries to have become like a single entity.

The ultimate in civilization has entailed the transmission of information by a form of magnetism called the telegraph, which is among the wonders of the world and is evidence of the influence of pure science growing up in the cradle of security nourished by the milk of freedom. The English even laid a cable in the Great Ocean (Atlantic), but it broke. They returned to the work. It broke again, and they tried again. All this was from the private capital of the wealthy, not from state funds. This they did to seek profit from the transmitting of information. They now profit enormously from this. God knows best what is behind that which He prepares for humanity.

(58) This step-by-step approach has helped them achieve the development they sought and facilitated for them, without undue hardship, the means of civilization. That is to say, if the absolutely necessary is achieved in the best way, there can then follow attention to the necessary in a natural way of development. That being achieved, then one can seek the higher step of improvement, all being done progressively in accordance with what can be accepted and is ready. If they set their sights first on

achieving improvement, they would not reach that higher step. Experience makes this well-known.

Consider the telegraph in this Tunisian capital. Its income does not cover the payment of those operating it. Compare that with the telegraph in Europe. "He who hurries a thing before its time loses it." This is God's way with his creatures and his country.

The legal rules of the Europeans provide that their rulers are deemed above involvement in trying cases brought by litigants. This is to guard against possible injustice to the people, even if they should arrive at the correct judgment. In any case, reports of the trials and judgments from the criminal courts are forwarded to the rulers, who may then deign to pardon or lighten the sentences of those convicted or order execution of the sentence. The sentence is not carried out unless the ruler so orders. This is what is meant by the unity of judgment. It is not judgment according to the personal rule of one who should know how the eyes can deceive and the hearts conceal. Nor is it rejecting the help that comes from consultation. This would be the understanding of those who exclude from the constitution its very nature and purpose.

It is their custom not to increase the severity of punishment, for they treat their subjects like fathers with their sons. It is well known that the father, with his compassion, is not harsh with his son. Thus you find that while the punishments in the laws of the Franks are severe, especially military justice, because the aim is to deter the aggressor and to frighten others, there is hope for leniency by the rulers who are praised for their wisdom, compassion, and mercy, so much so that that subjects expect only that from their rulers. Stories are told of their great rulers, written in the chronicles and preserved in pages of official records. As is well known, kindness in daily acts is one of the highest values of the Religious Law. God Most High said to His Messenger, "Embrace forgiveness, command kindness and turn away from the ignorant" (Qur'an 7:199). And He has said, "Whosoever forgives and restores, his portion is from God, who does not love oppressors" (Qur'an 42:40). Muhammad, may God bless him and grant him peace has said, (59) "God has mercy on the merciful." And he said, "Be merciful to those of this world and He who is in heaven will be merciful to you." Among the sayings of the wise are, "the kindness of rulers preserves their rule," "gentleness is the key to victory and the seed of success," and "haste in punishment debases the victory." There are many other such customs, sayings, and maxims. Indeed, many of the ʿulama' assert, "Punishment beyond its proper limit is not permitted, and there should be an effort to find what is less than that." Yes, the Shariʿa punishments, on the face of them, are not subject to curtailment or pity, for they are as a cleansing for the violator and a repudiation of his sin, but they are to be held back when there is doubt. The truth about them rests with the Merciful, the Compassionate, may He be praised.

The custom of the Europeans concerning punishments is that should someone commit a crime not mentioned or covered by a ruling in the law consultation takes place to determine the punishment that will deter such a crime. If the ruler signs this judgment, then it becomes part of the law. The person having committed this crime is then given a lesser sentence because of his ignorance of the ruling, which was not yet part of the law. Others later are judged according to that ruling that has now become part of the law, which they would have reason to know. All the different aspects of the law are thus known, and a transgressor is aware of what will be imposed upon him for his criminal act. This is to escape the kind of independent judgment leading to absolute personal caprice. Praise to Him who said, "We never punish until we have sent a messenger" (Qur'an 17:15).

Among the reasons for the rulers being above the proceedings of the adversaries in court cases is that judgments are subject to being challenged—even if only *in camera*—by those possessing knowledge and good sense. The regal status of the rulers would not permit that they pursue such challenges except in general issues appropriate to their standing. Litigants accustomed to abusive language quite contrary to the propriety required in audiences with rulers would be so startled by the ruler's majesty as to fail to present their case as needed.

It is accepted and well known that delegating the trying of cases is not contrary to the Religious Law. It is not necessary that the imam personally preside over and decide cases between litigants.

ʿUmar ibn al-Khattab, may God be pleased with him, delegated Abu Darda' to serve as qadi with him in Madina. Later caliphs and rulers followed this precedent, since they were fully occupied with matters of the public interest that were much more important.

(60) It could be said that later autocratic and despotic rulers also did not personally decide cases between litigants. Instead, they appointed delegates from among the political judges and administrators, such as the head of the criminal court, the police chief (*sahib al-shurta*) and other such. In Tunis, however, the ruler personally presides over those cases, whether base or lofty, that he wishes to hear in the chamber known as the courtroom (*mahkama*).

Some chroniclers of these times dispute and exaggerate in disavowing this situation beyond what is the reality. I say: That took place only in the twelfth Hijri century. The earlier rulers of this country (Tunisia) from among the companions of the Prophet, then the followers and those who followed thereafter, were in a state of simplicity. Their concern was jihad to bring people to the religion of Islam and to preserve what had been conquered. And there were judges for the court cases.

The Aghlabids, when they gained power, were occupied with wars and Islamic conquests and beneficial questions and general issues with their Arab simplicity and a distancing from the haughtiness of rulers and refined customs of civilization. Their judges would sit in judgment over them and over their families and decide equitably between the people and them. Suffice it to mention judges like the imam Sahnun, who would accept public office only on the condition "if someone raised a case against any member of the Aghlabid family the person so charged would appear personally in court, not delegate someone else." This was a way of deterring them, for their pride would restrain them from that. Thus there would be no transgression from them, no repudiation of rights, and no action that might lead to a demand for justice in court. Sahnun personally served in the *hisba*[26] office with other qadis. He strove in the way of God to change the evil.

After them came the Fatimids, Banu ʿUbayd, who confronted the severity of their ʿulama', such as Ibn Abu Zayd al-Qayrawani, who made them to gulp down his bitterness. Their being occupied with wars, and spreading the *daʿwa* (proselytizing) in the countries, increasing their domains, and fighting the Abbasids prevented them from personally hearing cases between litigants. They supervised those whom they had delegated. The same held for their chosen successors, the Sanhaja. It was the same with the state of ʿAbd al-Mu'min ibn ʿAli and his sons in Morocco.

When rule came to the Hafsids, they followed this program. They aspired to achieve noble things and the characteristics and titles of the caliphate. They acted like the caliphs and they appointed others to serve as qadis, *mazalim* court judges, *muhtasibs*, and police. They called their appointees to account with a goodness, wisdom, justice, and equity like that of their earliest rulers. (61) The tenth sultan from among them even handed over his very own son to the qadi Ibn ʿAbd al-Rafiʿ. He was sentenced to death as punishment for having wrongly and aggressively killed an innocent person. If the legal guardians had not forgiven him, the punishment would have been carried out. Even so, the qadi imposed upon him as penance for the killing one year imprisonment and one hundred lashes in accordance with the Maliki legal school. He remained imprisoned until those of loosening and binding released him to receive the *bayʿa* when his father fled.

Such was their way that they would not permit themselves to waste time hearing quarrels and disputes among contenders in matters of embezzlement of a cow, horse, or sheep or the case of an uncouth bedouin girl who, after having been forbidden to marry by her father, had fled to her chosen suitor, or that of the debtor seized and languishing in prison until his debt is paid. Rulers haughtily disdained being asked to hear such cases. Rather, they concerned themselves with larger issues and the uprooting of injustice by choosing deputies and provincial governors and then monitoring their actions. They were, in any case, usually traveling to inspect how things were with their subjects. Seldom did their governors do what would cause complaints, for they were aware of the power restraining them. The ruler understood that the injustice of the follower accrues to the leader.

Their dynasty continued in this fashion until it, too, became afflicted with the illness of dynasties. The later rulers of the dynasty abandoned their favorable qualities and went astray with an animal-like abandon, not heeding the restraining force of either the Religious Law or reason. They became hemmed in by what they were doing, and dominion fell from their hands. God gives dominion to whomever he wishes from among his creatures.

When God liberated the country by the sword of the Ottoman Sultan Selim, may God have mercy on him, and the feet of his governors and valiant soldiers became firmly established, he created a force restraining the army. This was the offices of dey, pasha, and qadi.

The dey would render judgments in the gallery of the citadel (Qasba) in criminal matters and punish aggressors at all times, acting like a police chief. He could impose the death penalty. In his hand were the affairs of the country and its protection, in accordance with military might.

The pasha attended to the administration of the country and its people. Important legal cases were brought before him in the presence of the qadi and the two muftis (Hanafi and Maliki). He would execute what they decided upon. He who reads *al-Ajwiba al-ʿAdhumiyya* knows that, for it refers to the pasha and the two litigants. (62)

The bey was under the orders of the dey, and his authority came from him. He would go out to collect the taxes from the people of the hinterland and the like. He would govern them in a manner suitable to their savage and aggressive nature, for the country at that time suffered the wounds of preceding wars. There was not a back but that it was ridden and not a udder but that it was milked. The qadi judged cases of retribution and disputes between litigants. He had jurisdiction concerning orphans, those under guardians, the pious foundations, and the like.

Given what is known about the nature of the Turks with their respect for the Religious Law and their regard for its people (the ʿulama') and their staying within its bounds for the most part, you would not find one of them who would decide a litigation using his own judgment. It would only occur to him to imprison the debtor until he paid what he acknowledged that he owed. This was to ward off the injustice of delay. If, however, the debtor claimed incapacity, this was proved before the qadi in accordance with the principles of the Religious Law, and the debtor swore to it, the qadi would release him and the case would be moved from the injustice of postponing to the necessity of waiting. And they would often seek counsel concerning criminals, which would then result in their punishment.

When the Muradids came to power, they aspired to despotic rule and mastery over the deys. They conducted, in their stately homes in Tunis, some of the matters of administration, the punishment of bedouin criminals, and the complaints from their tribal appointees, in accordance with the offices of pasha and of bey that they held by sultanic order. They were much occupied with what was deemed most important to them, which was traveling to collect the taxes in the various parts of the country. They were traveling most of the year. Not one of them held court.

Husayn ibn ʿAli, the builder of the Husaynid dynasty, who came to power in Rabiʿ al-Awwal 1117 (July 1705), spent most of his time traveling to put out the fires of the remaining wars in the various parts of the country. He also led the summer and winter trips (*mahalla*) to collect taxes, the essential foundation of ruling authority. The dey known as al-Asfar (the yellow or pale one) was alienated from him and sought treacherously to assassinate him, but God saved him from the trap set. The bey then sought to free himself from the deys and to defeat them by winning over the hearts of the subjects, righting injustices done to them, acting against their oppressors, providing security in return for taxes, developing a mutually fond relationship with the army, and other such acts that attracted to him the hearts of the people. The deys became the chiefs of his police force. Their authority came from him, whereas before his authority was from them. He held court—whenever he was in the capital—in his house in the Tower Courtyard (*Sahn al-Burj*) at the Bardo Palace without pomp or splendor to hear those bringing complaints (63) against the provincial officials. He would render justice, doing the same regarding misdeeds of the bedouin and others. He would receive delegations from the villages and the tribes, indeed all who came to him, whether notables or those seeking alms, to such extent that he spent most of his days in that house, available to all who might seek him. He would not decide cases of retaliation but would refer them to the *Shariʿa* court, or for civil cases, refer the litigant to the *Sharʿi* court[27] or to the commercial court known as the Ten Notables or to the representatives of the farmers (*amins* of cultivation) or to the rabbis of the Jews if the dispute was between two Jews. He would see to it that justice was done, even in cases involving him. He appointed an agent from the Treasury to represent him in cases brought against him before the *Shariʿa* court in order to be just like the rest of the people.

Thus the matter continued, as we have come to know. His holding court in that house was his way of guarding against the destructiveness of the deys with resolution and love for the people of the country and a mixing with them. Most of his judgments ended to the satisfaction of the

two disputants or even by reconciliation, something he often recommended. He would say to those who might dislike it, "Wouldn't you prefer reconciliation, the lord of legal rulings?" Helping him in his aim to
defeat the deys was his being from among the people of the country, flesh
of their flesh, speaking their language. He loved the people, and they
inclined toward him given his gentleness, kindness, righteousness, and
modesty. He showed compassion for the weak and respect for the
ᶜulama'. Indeed, he honored the shaykh of Zitouna by going out of his
house to greet him and personally leading him into the house, for he was
blind. He did other such deeds of beneficence and integrity with a keen
intelligence and a mastery that comes from experience. This is because
he had practiced administration and held leadership positions in the days
of the Muradids. He had witnessed the wars and endured their harshness. He knew their causes and had seen with his own eyes the actions
that had caused the Muradids to perish quickly in the worst way. Thus,
his days were "like fertility after drought, peace after war and safety after
fear."[28] It is not remembered that he put to death a single person—except
in warfare—without either a proper fatwa or as decided before the members of the *Shariᶜa* court on the day they met with him. Customarily, the
qadi, after determining that it was necessary to impose the death penalty,
would summon the dey to execute the sentence. It once happened that
the qadi imposed the death sentence, but certain of the muftis disputed
this sentence. The qadi, even so, instructed the dey to carry out the sentence. The muftis then ordered him to stop, which he did, and informed
the bey. When the Majlis next met in his presence they discussed the case,
and it became clear that the man should not receive the death sentence.
The bey dismissed the qadi because of his haste and forbade the dey from
carrying out any sentence of amputation or death except by beylical
order. Moreover, that judgment would be rendered only by the *Shariᶜa*
court meeting with the bey. This procedure remained in effect. (64) Abu
ᶜAbd Allah Muhammad al-Shafiᶜi reported this more extensively in his
commentary on *Muharakat al-Sawakin*.

When his nephew ᶜAli Pasha ibn Muhammad came to power, he built
the court still existing at Bardo and he placed in it a quasi-imperial
throne. In his days it was called a court even though he would not try
cases involving *shariᶜa* transactions or punishments there. He would say,

"For such cases there are Religious *(Shar͑i)* or administrative *(siyasi)* judges," and he would hear complaints concerning the judges with what he had of specialized knowledge. He would attend to delegations, criminals, and those accused of rebelling against him and of favoring his cousins (the sons of Husayn Bey) who were in Algeria. He was reckless in shedding blood and would kill at the slightest suspicion. Stories about him continued to be told until fate summoned, the torrent flowed over him, and arrows of the night struck him. He also continued both the summer and winter tours (tax-collecting *mahalla*).

When the rule returned to the sons of Husayn Bey ibn ͑Ali in Dhu al-Hujja in 1169 (September 1756) the oldest, Muhammad Bey, changed the throne in the court to one more modest as a way of condemning his cousin (͑Ali Bey), with his tendency to haughtiness and vanity. This is the throne that we knew in the time of the later Muhammad Bey, who issued the *͑Ahd al-Aman* (Fundamental Pact). Muhammad Bey attended many sessions at court, spending the rest of his time in his garden in al-Manuba. He delegated his brother to lead the tax-collecting expeditions *(mahalla)* and to hold court. The minister and clerk, Hamuda ibn ͑Abd al-͑Aziz, in his history[29] describes the manner of his master, Pasha ͑Ali Bey ibn Husayn Bey, at court in calculating his exploits and regulations.

In it he shows the state of the country at that period. These rulers attended court largely to show the majesty of rulership, as a sign of their status, to receive the delegations from the Arab tribes and the countryside, and to hear the cases requiring punishment *(ta'zir)* such as brigandage and bedouin attacks, complaints against the provincial officials, and such like as pertain to the duties of the police chief and the *mazalim* courts. They would not consider *Shari͑a* cases of retaliation or transactions and the like, which would have required competence most of them did not possess. Indeed, those of good reputation among them did not take it upon themselves to attend court often. This was the case with Hamuda Pasha, who, at the beginning of his reign, followed the custom of his grandfather in extending his sessions in order to receive people, and he promulgated his permission to receive those complaining of oppression. (65) He would often permit those standing to the left and the right to leave with only the clerks, the *bash hamba*, and a few unavoidable hangers-on remaining. Then toward the end of his reign, he curtailed his sessions considerably when he realized that those bringing complaints sought to force the objects of their complaints into court, which entailed paying the resulting costs—an appreciable source of income for the *mukhazaniyya*[30] who brought in the accused.

A bedouin approached the bey with a complaint against a fellow bedouin and the bey said, "I appointed a provincial governor [*qa'id*] for you. Take such cases to him." The bedouin replied, "I did raise my case with him, but he did not give me justice against my adversary." The bey then stated, "Now your complaint is against the *qa'id*. Take my order to him that he is to present himself here with you." When the *qa'id* arrived the plaintiff acknowledged that his purpose had been to have his adversary summoned.

If the accused before the bey said, "I appeal to God and the noble *shari͑a*" then he would force the accuser to appear before a *shari͑a* court. If one of the evildoers were to say to the bey "You are the head of *shari͑a* justice or the chief judge [*qadi*]," he would reply, "they are my delegates." And often he would say to anyone who would understand the speech, "If you do not submit voluntarily you will fall into apostasy." He knew the meaning of monarchy and the meaning of court.

This is different from what happened after him. The meaning of monarchy to them was the magnificence of the court and greatness of receptions, so much so that Husayn Bey despised hearing lowly complaints. He would drive out anyone complaining of oppression, turning him over to the dey or other holding authority in the country, preserving thereby the marks of greatness.

͑Ali ibn Hilal al-Manisi, one of the notables of the ͑Adah Bashiyya tribe, who was an impatient man, came to him during Ramadan to complain about a butcher who served a customer who had actually arrived after him. I was that day among the clerks with the bey. After the man had finished his statement, the bey, who realized that the complaint was intended to cause the butcher to be summoned and then required to pay the costs, replied: "You were raised in the court and you know its dignity. Do you presume to raise this complaint before it? Do you deem me to be the head of the butcher's guild? Or of the welfare fund? [*amin al-ma͑ash*]?" The bey ordered him to be imprisoned to teach him a lesson. The Bash Hamba then told the bey: "This man as you know is impatient.

He swore that if he did not bring this matter to your eminence he would divorce his wife. He then brought the complaint lest he be obliged to divorce his wife." The man was freed even before he reached the prison.

This is the situation of the court and the kinds of sentences that come from it as a rule. Except that the situation in these recent days—the last forty years—has become such as to violate all reason and custom. Indeed, those notables coming from Europe stamped with a (66) love of justice and desiring knowledge often ask permission to attend court, keen as they are to learn of things. They are amazed. They see the one seeking justice being held by two persons. He presents his complaint while standing before a ruler dressed in a lion's skin seated on a royal throne. Before him are two rows of angels[31] of wrath. One person of special importance presents his complaint, standing no farther than a spear's length from the judge. Another, lacking any rank, presents his complaint several steps removed, social status being the standard of ranking and justice. The Europeans see cases being decided in minutes, at times by accepting the truthfulness of the litigant—especially if he is one of the officials—and at other times by relying on what he calls his case. At times the litigant is seized even before he can open his mouth and those angels of wrath standing before the judge snatch him away when they hear him trying to speak. At times they even stop up the defendant's mouth with their hands if he tries to shout an answer. Their chief, the *bash hamba,* so orders them if he deems there is any lack of propriety. The Europeans will see that the charges are not written to be seen or heard by the defendant so that he might be able to respond. Rather the chief clerk, or whoever is taking his place at court, will examine the charge and give the judge the gist of the matter. The Europeans will urgently ask about these and other such events and they will not be convinced by the erroneous answers given, for they are characterized by a longing to know about and understand things.

Ahmad Bey was informed of the remonstrances of the Europeans, and this was one of the reasons that turned him against presiding at court. He greatly reduced his attendance at court, to such extent that he was blamed for this. The ignorant thought it was out of neglect on his part, but the true reason for his withdrawal was what he, with his penetrating intelligence and attentiveness, had learned about countries having a constitution and his inclination to follow what God had impressed upon him of freedom, especially after the promulgation of the Noble Rescript ushering in the *Tanzimat*. He had responded to that with what was required of hearing and obeying. With his mental acuity and loftiness of soul, he understood the secrets of the *Tanzimat*, especially after his trip to Paris where he witnessed himself what he might otherwise have thought to be exaggerated.

One day Mustafa Sahib al-Tabi^c, the virtuous and counseling minister who had educated him, censured him, saying, "The people maintain that you are neglecting public affairs by failing to attend sessions at court." Ahmad Bey replied: "What neglect has occurred O my father? I have delegated Khayr al-Din Kahiya to preside over these cases at the Bardo gallery and to oversee bringing disputants from the villages and pasturages of the bedouin. I have appointed the dey in Tunis to hold court as well. And the *Shar^ci* court decides the cases of transactions and punishment and it is for me to execute *Shar^ci* judgments. I consider my presiding over court, as was the custom of my father and grandfather, does not accord with the situation of these times. Such is the basis of justice of the French (67) in Algeria and the *Tanzimat* in Tripoli, Cairo, and Alexandria, and the Hijaz." You will see other such things related, God willing, in this chronicle.

I have expatiated on this matter of judging between disputants in court because many people see it as the elixir of justice, the fountainhead of prosperity, the meaning of governance and the soul of administration with its many benefits not reached except by crossing that bridge. The best of rulers is he who persuades even though he is capable of imposing, who takes pains to do justice both in secret and openly. He who controls himself can control others.

One of the branches of the constitution among Europeans is a consultative assembly composed of notables and the intellectuals of the state elected by the people. The composition of the assembly, the manner of electing its members, the conditions governing the elected and the electors, and the number of its members may vary according to the conditions and customs of the countries. This assembly is the people's representative. They are elected to protect their human rights (*huquq insaniyya*) and to defend them, but without rebelling.

The greatest of their rights is the constitution that they sacrificed themselves to obtain. It is the pivot around which revolves the security of their lives, wealth, and dignity. Whatever that assembly does is valid for all of the people, for what the delegate does is incumbent on the delegator.

By means of this delegation, the assembly is permitted to question the ministers and to oppose them, which is—but for this veil of propriety—to oppose the rulers. For the ministers are the agents of these rulers. The assembly may even demand the dismissal of ministers should they take actions violating the constitution because the commitment is upon them, not upon the rulers. In this way the necessary majesty, esteem and decorum of the ruler remains as it should be.

Certain judicious rulers, whose good sense triumphs over their passions, impose this commitment upon themselves, not just on their ministers. This is the case of the ruler of France at this time, Louis Napoleon III, and he puts up with the severe criticism of those notables such as the famous author and philosopher, Thiers, something that only his love of justice and of country make bearable.

(68) This, however, might well be difficult for those representing the people, because to oppose the minister—who is a delegate—is not like opposing the ruler. His status in that country is like that of a father. It is appropriate that the ministers be reproached, for they possess security and freedom just like the generality of the people, unlike those wretched ministers mentioned earlier in the first section on absolute rule caught between the lion's claw and the fang.

The situation of this assembly resembles the constitution of Sultan Sulayman, mentioned earlier, in preempting the excuse by giving due notice. For this reason there are few rebellions against rulers in Europe, because the ruler, if he ascertains from the assembly—which is the spokesman for the people—a disposition to rebel, he does not push them to it but shows the restraint of a father to his son in order to avoid disobedience. May God show His mercy to the father who helps his son in righteousness.

Such an assembly is thus worthy of esteem accorded to the Islamic Religious Law for it unifies opinion and avoids differences in the community, brings love between the ruler and the ruled, and spares bloodshed and wealth. By it are achieved the blessings and benefits such as were reaped in the early days of Islam, when there was a concern to forbid the evil as mentioned in Islamic books. God determines how things turn out. All praise to Him who has no need for a minister or a counselor. "He is not to be asked about what He does. He is the all wise, the all aware" (Qur'an, first sentence from 21:23, second 6:73, and elsewhere).

It is God's way, as Ibn Khaldun has said, that kingdoms do not follow the well-ordered way unless the dynasty can both issue orders and be called to account. The constitutional dynasty is authoritative, having royal rights and held to account by the constitutional rights imposed on it. In such circumstances, the dynasty is required to seek what is needed from those qualified and elect those possessing knowledge and experience and not put forward out of favoritism anyone whose actions would demonstrate his inadequacy. For the wise prefer experience over guesswork and examination over idle choice and other such beneficial means producing prosperity to the country and probity to its people. Praised be Him who said, "God brought you forth from the wombs of your mothers knowing nothing, and gave you hearing, sight, and hearts that you may give thanks" (Qur'an 16:78).

The learned one of the community and the pride of imams, Shaykh al-Islam ʿArif Bey, of lofty reputation, discussed this matter with me when I traveled to Islambul (Istanbul) in the beginning of the year 1258 (February 1842) as a member of the traveling party of the eminent elderly shaykh Khayr al-Din Kahiya (69) as Ahmad Bey's emissary to the Sublime State. This was during the reign of Sultan ʿAbd al-Majid Khan, may God's mercy be upon him, who had promulgated the previously mentioned Noble Rescript. The minister [grand vizier] at that time was Muhammad ʿIzzat Pasha. Our visit concerned the *Tanzimat*. The minister said, "Sayyid ʿArif Bey wants a word with you." He was at that time a member of the Consultative Council. When I met with him, he talked to me about the *Tanzimat* and its benefits, of the circumstances facing the Muhammadan umma who had fallen prey to the tyranny of ruler and officials, and other such matters.

I said to him, "It is difficult to implement the beneficial *Tanzimat* in the hinterlands of the Maghrib." I clarified for him the reasons in a speech that I thought would convince him. He responded that the

Tanzimat is a means of offering security to the people in their lives, wealth, and dignity. Thus, every means for reaching that security is to be sought.

There was much talk with him on this subject. Then he said in the presence of notables, "I implore you by God and His Prophet, do you see it as reasonable and in accordance with tradition that the caliph of God's prophet was bound in his actions by a constitution that he could not ignore and yet your master [the bey] is unbound in his actions, can do whatever he pleases and rules as he wishes?" I replied, "He is bound by the Religious Law (*Sharīʿa*) and by the public interest as set by existing circumstances."

He then asked, "Is he impeccable?" I answered, "No." And he said, "God ordered the impeccable to consult in the matter." I said, "He consults his men and his confidants." He then asked, "Do they have the power to force him to do the right should he violate it?" And he did not demand an answer from me, because he wanted to save me from telling a lie or exaggerating. Then he told me: "This is a matter embraced by the believer who turns for advice to God, His prophet, and the imams, as well as the generality of the Muslims, and it is hated by rulers who love to share with God, great is His majesty, in not being asked about what they do and with no obstacle to their judgments. It is also hated by advisors to such rulers, who prefer their personal fortunes over the public interest such as those provincial governors who had the claws of their crimes sundered by the sword of the *Tanzimat*. In a part of Anatolia there took place from the populace what resembled a revolt. They were saying in their ignorance, 'The *Tanzimat* is a new religion. God's religion is Islam.' It was agreed that they were to be fought, but I said to those assembled, 'Before doing that we must excuse and warn,' and I asked permission to go to them. The sultan so ordered, and I went to their villages and I sat on their pulpits and summoned the people group by group. I read the Noble Rescript to them and showed them the evidence of its sources in the Religious Law. I repeated to them these clarifications until they understood. It was then as if they were freed from their fetters and they called out for victory and support to their sultan (70) [This is the essence of what he said.] I thus realized that when right comes forward and the bad is destroyed, when the gates of tyranny are closed in their faces, then the officials influence their associates to spread the satanic whispers of evil among the people to such extent that they say what they say. 'And God was sufficient for the believers in their fight' (Qur'an 33:25). And when I returned, the sultan asked me and I said, 'Yes, the sultan and the subjects will be delighted and the officials wretched. The situation is set aright only by advancing trustworthy officials. And the best are not cut off from the umma.' And I presented the necessary advice."

Then ʿArif Bey said to me after his speech, "What is it in the *Tanzimat* that you reject?"

I answered him, "I do not refuse the Sultan anything."

Then he said, "Answer me according to what you know of religious sciences, not according to your ties to your master [the bey]." The normal rules of polite discourse required that I respond accordingly.

I said, "May God give you strength. You had only wished to prevail in order to do so."

And he said, "So, you will not do me justice?"

I said, "If you deem me qualified to do so, then I must."

He said: "God has no need for a vizier or a counselor. He is the first cause, the freely choosing. He consulted the angels about Adam, God's blessings upon him. He heard their objections, and He answered them." And he discussed the commentary of the sufi shaykh, Ismaʿil Haqqi, which was among the books that he had with him. He read from it the words of God, "And when God said to the angels I am about to place a vice-regent [khalifa] on the earth" (Qur'an 2:30). This, he continued, "had the advantage of teaching consultation on matters before implementing them, even though He in His knowledge and wisdom had no need for consultation. And He gave greater importance to the matter of what is to be done by announcing Adam to the inhabitants of His realm and entitling him vice-regent [khalifa] even before creating him and showing His preponderant favor to Adam. Wisdom requires that in which the good predominates. To abandon a great good in order to avoid a small evil is a great evil. Other such things are mentioned in the commentary on the noble verse."

Then he said, "A later foreign scholar has concerned himself to interpret that verse in a good collection." He then related from memory the essence of that commentary, revealing his excellent memory and knowledge of the subject. A part of what he said was: (71)

> God's ordinances are implemented in various ways. God imposed consultation upon his Lofty Self and those He had created in order that rulers would not disdain its use, for the world of the ruler is like that of the heavenly kingdom and if the Creator, may He be praised, did not deem Himself above consultation, how then can the creature be? Consider how He consulted His creatures first. Then he guided His messenger, whom He endowed with a great character in saying "If you had been rough and hard-hearted they would have dispersed from around you. Pardon them and ask forgiveness for them and consult about the conduct of affairs. And when you have resolved, then trust in God" (Qur'an 3:159). This commentary maintains that the counselor is to be entrusted with his opinion even if he might appear to be rude or if counselors answer the ruler in a questioning and rejecting manner. Consultation requires a discussion that might appear to be argumentative. This is deduced from another Qur'anic verse as the Almighty instructed Muhammad to say, "I had no knowledge of the exalted chiefs when they contended" (Qur'an 38:69). Also, Adam, in giving things their names, exercised an active, outgoing knowledge, different from the individual passivity or praising and glorifying God, leading to intimacy and love. Moreover, among the benefits and blessings of consultation is that broaching a well-known issue offers thoughtful consideration before implementation. Also refinement of the right is among the potentialities of thought. This is the way to extract the fruit of intelligences and win over hearts for work.

He raised other such matters in that evening's conversation, which my memory fails in being able to recall. God "grants wisdom to whom He wishes" (Qur'an 2:269).

I have expatiated in this matter of kingship, but this may not be lacking in benefit. Prolixity may be necessary given the present standing of history. Many of our colleagues do not think well of it and consider it a blameworthy innovation (*bidʿa*) in Islam. Yet, one should know that there are some innovations that are necessary. Moreover, they deem writing history to be copying the ways of non-Muslims.[32] Even if one were to grant this, should the believers be deprived of that which is good and beneficial, that which cannot be disavowed? Wisdom is the goal of the believer. He gathers it wherever he finds it. There are other examples of things said only to flatter rulers. "Every soul is held in pledge for what it has earned" (Qur'an 74:38). May God have mercy on Abu Ishaq al-Shatibi, who said, "We have seen that failure to compromise when the times call for compromise leads to corruption, yea to corruptions, even more contrary to the Religious Law." And "God guides who He wishes to the straight path" (Qur'an 2:213 and 22:46).

CHAPTER SIX

Conclusion

MENTIONING SOMETHING OF WHAT IS TO BE FOUND IN JUSTICE
AND CONSULTATION AND THE TRAITS OF THE JUST IMAM AND
OTHER SUCH THINGS THAT IMPROVE THE ASSEMBLIES OF RULERS

(72) God Most High said: "O David, we have made you a caliph on earth.
Judge the people with righteousness. Do not follow desire, lest it lead you
astray from God's way" (Qur'an 38:26). And God Most High said, "If you
judge, judge among them fairly. God loves the equitable" (Qur'an 5:42).
Sufficient for you is what leads to the love of God and His creatures.

And Muhammad, may God bless him and grant him peace, said,
"Those most loved by God are those who most love the people." And
ʿUmar ibn al-Khattab, may God be pleased with him, said, "Love of
God's creatures leads to love of God, and hatred of them to hatred of
God, for they are God's witnesses to His creation." And ʿUmar said to
one of his officials: "The people in truth are equal. Do not hold back
your love for the people. The prophets were examined concerning their
love for the people. If God loves a creature then you love him, and if He
hates a creature then you hate him. Consider that your standing with
God is as that with the people."

Al-Qurtubi relates in *al-Tadhkira*, "The just iman will be in paradise
with the prophets, the righteous, and the martyrs."

Muhammad, may God bless him and grant him peace, said, "Those
who act justly will be on pulpits of light on the day of resurrection." He
also said, "There are three whose prayers will not be rejected: the just

imam, the one who fasts the canonical limit, and the oppressed seeking justice, whom God will lift up (73) above the clouds and open for him the gates of heaven." And God most high says, "My glory and majesty will cause you to triumph, even if only after a while."[1] And Muhammad, may God bless him and grant him peace, said, "Do you know who of those from past times will be in God's shadow on the day of resurrection?"

"God and the prophet know," those hearing him answered.

He then said, "Those who, when given the truth, accept it and when examined, act on it. So judge the people as they judge themselves." And Muhammad, may God bless him and grant him peace, said, "Justice is the glory of the faith, and with it, the righteousness of rule. It is the strength of the notables and the people. By it is achieved the people's prosperity and security."

The proof of Islam, al-Ghazali, relates in his book *Nasihat al-Muluk* (Advice to Rulers) that the prophet, may God bless him and grant him peace, said, "There is not a creature whom God charged with the affairs of the subjects and then deceived them, failed to consult them or show concern for them but that God forbade him paradise." And Muhammad, may God bless him and grant him peace, said, "Whosoever is charged with the affairs of the Muslims and does not protect them just as he protects his own family, let a place be prepared for him in hell."

The author of the *ʿIqd al-Farid* has related, "When Umar ibn ʿAbd al-ʿAziz became caliph, he asked Hasan al-Basri, may God be pleased with him, to write for him the characteristics of the just imam." He wrote to him as follows:

> Know, O Commander of the Faithful, that God made the just imam the straightener of what leans, the goal of anyone who is perplexed, the restorer of whatever is corrupt, strengthener of the weak, justice for the oppressed, and a refuge for the troubled. The just imam is like the shepherd concerned for his flocks, who seeks out for them the best pastures and defends them against breeding grounds of destruction, protects them from beasts of prey, and shelters them from the harm of heat and cold. The just imam, O Commander of the Faithful, is like the father compassionate for his children. He works for them when they are young and teaches them as they are grow up. He earns what they need during his life-

time and saves for what will be theirs after his death. The just imam, O Commander of the Faithful, is like the compassionate mother devoted and tender to her son. She bears the distress of her pregnancy and his birth. She raises him as a child. She watches over him in his sleeplessness and her repose is in his repose. She suckles him and then weans him. She rejoices in his good health and grieves in his suffering. The just imam, O Commander of the Faithful, is the guardian of orphans, the treasurer of the poor. He raises those who are young and provides for those who are old. The just imam, O Commander of the Faithful, is like the heart within the body that thrives when it thrives and decays when it decays. The just imam, O Commander of the Faithful, stands between God and His creatures. He hears the word of God and causes the people to hear. He looks to God and causes them to see. He is led to God and leads them to God.

So, with the authority God has given you, O Commander of the Faithful, do not be like the slave whom the master entrusted to guard over his wealth and family, only to have him squander his master's wealth and drive away his family. Know, O Commander of the Faithful, that God sent down the canonical limits to restrain (74) wickedness and obscenities. How can the one placed in charge commit them? God sent down the canonical punishments to give life to his creatures. How can the one designated to implement the canonical punishments against the people kill the people himself?

Remember, O Commander of the Faithful, death and what follows death when your followers and supporters will be few. Prepare yourself for it and for the great terror that follows. Know, O Commander of the Faithful, that there is for you a place other than what you have now. It will long be your dwelling place. Your loved ones will leave you in its pit, alone and solitary. So provide yourself with what will accompany you on "the day in which a man will flee from his brother, his mother, his father, his wife, and his sons" (Qur'an 80:34–36). Remember, O Commander of the Faithful, "when the contents of the graves are brought forth and the secrets of the breasts are made known" (Qur'an 100:9–10). Secrets are manifest. The Book does not omit what is small or what is great. It counts all.

So now, O Commander of the Faithful, while you have the time before being overtaken by death and the end of your work, do not rule God's creatures as was done in the time of ignorance. Do not follow the path of the oppressors. Do not give the haughty power over the weak, for they treat the believer ruthlessly, lest you be made to bear your own sins and the sins of your wicked appointees and bear your own burdens and also the burdens of others.

Do not be deceived by those who enjoy what causes you distress and who devour the good things of this world of theirs by taking away the good things of your afterlife. Do not take thought of your fate today, but look to your fate the morrow. You are placed between the hands of God in the company of the angels, the prophets and the messengers. "And the faces will be humbled before the living, eternal God, and he who bears iniquity is indeed a failure" (Qur'an 20:111).

O Commander of the Faithful, even if I fail to reach in my admonition the extent reached by those earlier admonishers and fall short in my solicitude and advice, I bring you my letter as medicine treating a loved one, giving him to drink bitter medicine seeking from it vigor and health. Peace and God's mercy to the Commander of the Faithful.

Sa'd ibn Suwayd said: "Islam is a protecting wall and a secure gate. Its wall is righteousness and its gate justice. And Islam will remain well protected so long as the sultan acts severely, but the sultan's severity is not killing with the sword or blows with the lash, but judging with righteousness and acting with justice."

And among the maxims of the Persians: "Rulership is the foundation and justice the guard. What lacks a foundation is ruined. What lacks a guard is lost." Another maxim, "Justice is the strongest army and the most wholesome food."

(75) Aristotle wrote to Alexander: "Rule the subjects with beneficence. Conquer them with love. Your seeking that by your beneficence is more long-lived that by your coercion. Know that you possess the bodies. Bring together as well the hearts. Know that the subjects if able to speak are also able to act, so beware that the one unable to speak is free to act."

Walid ibn 'Abd al-Malik asked his father, "What is governance?" He replied, "It is leading the hearts of the subjects with just treatment to them and by abiding the mistakes of one's retinue."

The wise have said: "The ruler benefits only by his ministers and aides. The ministers and aides benefit only by friendship and advice. And friendship and advice are of benefit only with good opinion and integrity. Thus, rulers must not leave either the doer of a good deed or a bad without his just recompense. If they fail to do that, the good man becomes neglectful and the bad man bold. Then rule becomes corrupted and work stops."

In the *Advice To Rulers*: "The person in charge needs a thousand qualities, all of which can be assembled into two. If he acts according to them he is just. These are causing the country to prosper by bringing security to the inhabitants."

The wise have said: "The ruler's crown is his virtue. His citadel is his justice and his wealth his subjects. He must not use them to sharpen his sword or exceed the canonical limits in taking their wealth. To attack the people's wealth destroys their hopes, and if hope vanishes, work stops."

And the wise have said, "He who imposes upon his subjects taxation exceeding their capacity is like one who uses the clay of the foundation of his house to cover the roof."

And from among the collections of what Muhammad, may God bless him and grant him peace, said, "Forgiveness increases a creature's might and modesty increases his standing."

And the wise said, "The ruler's forgiveness causes his rule to endure."

ʿAli ibn Abu Talib, may God be pleased with him, said, "He who is honorable will scorn his appetites. He who is self-satisfied increases anger against him. And he who does what he wishes will find what is wicked."

The wise have said, "Kindness is the key to success, and he who is closest to forgiveness is the most able to punish and he who is most concerned with good works is most deserving of God's recompense."

(76) It is said, "Swiftness of punishment is the wickedness of victory and victory over the weak is a defeat."

It is said: "The most lacking in intelligence is he who oppresses his inferior. The ruler does not need to oppress. By him oppression is to be eliminated."

It is said, "If you oppress your inferior you will not be safe from the punishment of your superior."

It is said, "The subordinate's oppression redounds to the superior."
ᶜUmar ibn al-Khattab, may God be pleased with him, said, "If anyone
brings me a complaint against an official, and I do not make it right, then
I am his oppressor." And he said, "As you wish God to do to you, so do
you to your subjects."

Muhammad, may God bless him and grant him peace, has said,
"The fastest of things is the punishment of injustice."

And the wise have said: "There is no abundance for him whom injustice gives abundance, no strength for him whom oppression strengthens
and no dominion for him whom usurpation has given dominion. Dominion
and injustice never come together on the same throne but that it becomes
empty."

Muhammad, may God bless him and grant him peace, said, "Consultation is a citadel guarding against remorse and a security against
blame."

And in the traditions, "He who rejects advice will see disgrace."

It is said: "He who enlightens you saves you, and he who warns you
awakens you. He who is content with his own counsel is endangered and
whoever asks advice is on the brink of success."

Muhammad, may God bless him and grant him peace, said, "He
who values his own opinion makes mistakes and he who lords it over
people is contemptible."

ᶜAli ibn Abi Talib, may God be pleased with him, said, "There is no
poverty more severe than ignorance and no wealth mightier than intelligence and no estrangement more severe than vanity."

And the wise said, "Vanity is the gate that bars man from the right
path."

ᶜAmru ibn al-ᶜAs said, "There is no authority without men and no
men without wealth, no wealth without cultivation and no cultivation
without justice."

In the same sense is the famous circle from the wise men of Persia:
"The world is a garden whose enclosure is the state, the state is the authority animated by the tradition, the tradition is the sound policy conducted
by the kingdom, the kingdom is the system (77) protected by the soldiers,
the soldiers are the protectors supported by wealth, wealth is the property gathered by the subjects, the subjects are the slaves bound by justice,

justice is the balance supporting the world, and the world is a garden whose enclosure is the state." Those eight politic and aphoristic words are linked one to the other, unbroken. They are bound together into a closed circle. Consider the phrase "bound by justice," for justice is strongest of reasons for devotion that can bind the free.

There is the maxim "I wondered about the man who purchased slaves with his money. Why will he not purchase the free with his actions?"

The Shaykh al-Islam, Muhammad ibn al-Khuja,[2] has a pleasant and precious commentary to explain the "circle," which he composed at the request of Ahmad Bey early in his reign.

We have related in this conclusion the fundamentals upon which are built the laws of rulers regardless of their community or location. On advice to rulers and on governance there are many famous books written by the most notable possessors of knowledge and piety. We have taken from these rivers a drop for the tip of our pen so that the observer may see in these few lines how people should be governed. "God created you and what you make" (Qur'an 37:96).

In sum, the basis of the matter is to be found in the sermon of the shaykh of the rightly-guided caliphs, "the second of two when the they were together in the cave,"[3] Abu Bakr al-Siddiq, may God be pleased with him, upon his taking office, which was very much like the oath of constitutional rulers. Let us mention as the crowning touch[4] its text:

> O people, I am empowered to rule over you, but I am not better than you. If you see me doing what is right, appoint me, and if you see me doing what is wrong, resist me. Obey me as long as I obey God, and if I disobey Him, then I hold no right to your obedience. The strongest of you in my eyes is the one who is weak until receiving the right due him. The weakest of you is the strong one until the right not his due is taken from him. I say this and ask God's pardon for me and for you.

You see how he linked obedience due him to his obedience to God concerning them. And obedience to God entails their rights, the greatest of which is justice achieved by means of him. Justice is the substance of the law, as has been shown. God is the guardian of the believers.

Here ends the first part of the Introduction.

CHAPTER SEVEN

The 1857 Fundamental Pact
The ʿAhd al-Aman

The ʿAhd al-Aman, promulgated in Tunis on 10 September 1857, is deemed to have been largely based on the earlier Ottoman Hatt-ı Şerif of Gulhane (Noble Rescript in this translation) of 1839, but a comparison of the two texts will show that the ʿAhd al-Aman is much more concerned with spelling out rights to foreign residents in the country. (See translation pp. 84-87.) Not surprising, that, since four days earlier both the British and French consuls had sent letters to the Tunisian government suggesting what needed to be included in the text.

Praise be to God, Who opened a way to the truth and made justice a guarantor to preserve the organization of the world and sent down the judgments appropriate to the interests of the people and promised the just and warned the unjust. Whose word is better than that of God? Prayers and peace be upon our master Muhammad, whom God in His Book praised as kind and merciful and gave him preference. He sent him with the true and tolerant religion. He revealed it. He made clear its meaning. He arranged it as his Master ordered in the permissible, the recommended, the forbidden, and the legitimate.[1] You will not find in God's *sunna* any change. You will not find in God's custom any modification. Prayers and peace upon Muhammad's family and his companions, who established on the signposts of right guidance the knowledge needed for those who would be guided. They caused the Religious Law to be understood in text and interpretation. They have left behind their noble lives

131

and their just rulings as a glorious trust (*aman*). We ask of You, O God, to grant us success in what pleases You and to support us in conducting the affairs of governing, a heavy burden upon whomever bears them. We have placed our trust in You and seek refuge in You. And God is sufficient as guarantor.

The authority that God has bestowed upon us and His charging us to govern His people in this country imposes on us necessary duties, both legally binding as well as supererogatory religious obligations that we are able to perform only with His support on Whom we rely. Without such support, who could ever fulfill the duties due to God and to His people?

In sincere support of God's prescriptions concerning His creatures, His land, and His country, and in the hope that there will not remain among them oppression or long-suffering, I will not disturb in any way the proper ordering of their rights. How can anyone who realizes that "God does not harm even the weight of a dust particle" (Qur'an 4:40) and does not love the oppressor in His creation, deviate from that goal in either his actions or intentions? God said to his impeccable prophet, who turned always to Him: "O David! We have made you a vice-regent [*khalifa*; caliph] on the earth. Therefore, judge aright between men. And do not follow desire lest it beguile you from the way of God. Those who wander from the way of God have an awful doom because they forget the day of reckoning" (Qur'an 38:26).

God is my witness that in accepting this rule, with all its seriousness, I have preferred the interests of the country (*watan*) above my own. I have spent the great part of my time in its service in thought and action. I have already begun the lessening of the tax burden as is known, and the impact of this, with God's help, is to be seen. Hopes have increased and the people anticipate the fruits of their labor. The hands of the officials have been restrained from transgression. To get to the root of securing the public interests requires comprehensiveness, but he who seeks this all at once risks, because of the difficulties involved, neglecting something.

We have seen that the majority of the people of this country (*qatar*) lack assurance about what we have intended to do. It is God's custom that people do not achieve prosperity unless they know that they are assured of security and protection. Having secured this shield of justice removes from a person the fear of aggression. Only strong evidence and clear proof should tear the curtain of his inviolability, not just one or two witnesses.

If the guilty confronts many witnesses he will, if he is reasonable, correct his assumption that he can escape the charge and say, "He who goes beyond God's limits does harm to himself" (Qur'an 65:1).

We have seen the rulers of Islam and the great powers, who are most distinguished in their worldly politics, guarantee security to the subject. They see it as among the inalienable rights approved by both reason and nature. This is also what the *Sharīʿa* bears witness to, for it came to extract the responsible person (*mukallaf*) from the temptation of caprice. He who embraces justice and vows to uphold it is the most God-fearing. By security are hearts made confident and strengthened.

We have already written to the important ʿulama' of the community (*milla*) and to certain of the notables telling them of our resolve to establish important councils (*majlis*-s) to look into all manner of crimes as well as commerce, which is the wealth of nations (*buldan*). And we have established in these arrangements that which, God willing, does not violate *Sharīʿa* rules.

The *Sharīʿa* rules, may God magnify them, are in effect and obeyed. And may God cause them to continue until the Hour.

This political law (*al- qanun al-siyasi*) requires a certain amount of time to produce its teachings and to be organized and refined. I ask of God, who looks into our hearts, that by this law the circumstances of leadership will be well established and that it will not violate the sound policies that have come from the pious ancestors (*al-salaf al-salih*). I, the humble servant of God, hasten to accomplish what will please my Master and assure the souls of the people. May it have in the hearts of the people the standing of a matter that is seen and felt. It is founded on the following bases:

1. The assurance of protection to all of our subjects and the inhabitants of our country (*iyala*)[2] without regard to their religion, language, or color. Their honored bodies are to be respected, their wealth inviolate, and their honor esteemed, the only exception being cases duly brought to court and reviewed by us. We will reserve the right to sign the sentence, or reduce it or return it for review.

2. Complete equality of all inhabitants in matters of existing or future taxation, however they might differ in amount. The tax law is not to exempt the grand because of his greatness or impose on the lowly because of his lowliness. And the tax will be clearly announced.

3. Equality between the Muslim and others from among the inhabitants of the country (iyala) in their right to justice. This is because the right to justice derives from one's common humanity, not any other distinction. Justice in this world is the equal balance by which right prevails against wrong and the weak against the strong.

4. The dhimmis from among our subjects will not be forced to change their religion and will not be prevented from carrying out their religious duties. Their places of worship will not be despised. They will have protection from all harm or disrespect. This is because their status as dhimmis requires that they have what we have and there can be imposed on them only what is imposed on us.

5. Since the army guarantees the security of all and what is in their interests extends to all, and since a man needs the time to arrange his livelihood and attend to his family, we will recruit soldiers only in an orderly fashion and by lot. Nor will the soldier remain in service for longer than an announced period as will be fixed in a military code.

6. For any judgment in the criminal court against one of the dhimmis, someone from among their leaders, whom we will appoint, must be present. This is to put them at ease and to ward off what they might expect of partiality. The Shari'a counsels that they be well treated.

7. We will establish a commercial court with a judge, clerk, and members including Muslims and others from among the subjects of friendly states, to consider commercial cases. After agreement with our friends, the great powers, concerning the modalities of putting their subjects under the jurisdiction of the court, clarification of the details to prevent any controversy will be issued.

8. All of our subjects, Muslim and others, are equal in matters of customary law ('urfiyya) and other laws in existence. There is to be no favoritism given anyone over another.

9. Commerce is to be freed from monopoly by anyone. It will be open to all. The regime (dawla) will not engage in trade and will

not prevent others from doing so. The concern will be to aid in facilitating commerce and to prevent whatever disrupts it.

10. Those who come to our country (*iyala*) have the right to engage in any industry or service on condition that they comply with laws that now exist or may be enacted just like all the inhabitants of the country. There is to be no preference for any one of them over another following our agreement with their states concerning the modality of their being integrated into this, as will be later announced.

11. Subjects of all countries coming to our country (*iyala*) have the right to purchase houses, gardens, and lands just like all inhabitants of the country (*bilad*) provided they follow, without exceptions, the laws enacted or that may be enacted. There is to be no difference in the least matter of the laws of the land (*bilad*). We will, after our agreement with friendly states, make clear later the modalities of habitation so the owner will know what he is to obey.

I swear by God's promise and His covenant to implement these principles that we have signed just as we have indicated and we will make clear their meaning. I bear witness before God and this august gathering, which we salute, that I and my successors will be entitled to rule only by swearing to uphold the pledge of security (*aman*) for which I have exerted myself. I make the delegates of the great powers and the notables from among our subjects witnesses to my commitment (*ʿahd*). God knows that this goal, which I have made known and that I have brought together these notables to explain, is what God placed within me. To carry out its roots and branches immediately is greatest of my aspirations. What is required of one is his best effort. Whosoever has pledged to God must fulfill his pledge. Justice is "the firmest bond" (Qur'an 2:256, 31:22). The afterlife is better and more lasting (Qur'an 87:17).

I exact the oath from those in whom I have confidence and are able, that they will be as one hand with me in carrying out this public interest, that they do this with hearts sound and supportive. I say to them, "Do not violate the oath after it is taken. Verily you have made God a guarantor. Truly, God knows what you do" (Qur'an 16:91).

O God, support those who have helped us for the interests of Your creatures. Bring down on them the flowing fresh waters of Your grace. O

God, support us with Your providence and Your assistance. Grant us Your mercy and prepare for us a clear way in this matter we pursue. Our help in what You have entrusted us comes from You. Rightly guided is he whom You have guided. All good exists in what You have decreed.

This beginning (*muqaddima*) has been produced by consultation, and Your humble creature has seen it to be favorable and sound. O God help us with the blessing of the Qur'an and the secrets of the *Fatiha* (opening chapter of the Qur'an).

Salutations from the servant of God Almighty, His creature, Marshal Muhammad Pasha Bey, ruler of the Tunisian kingdom (*mamlaka*) on the twentieth of Muharram al-Haram at the opening of the year 1274 (10 September 1857).

Notes

INTRODUCTION

1. This is the work that I translated almost four decades ago: *The Surest Path: The Political Treatise of a Nineteenth–Century Muslim Statesman.* Harvard Middle East Monograph 16 (1967).

2. Ibn Khaldun, *The Muqaddimah: An Introduction to History.* Trans. Franz Rosenthal, 2nd ed. 3 vols. Princeton, NJ: Princeton University Press, 1967.

3. One could well add to this comparative historical schema the two independent Muslim states just beyond the Ottoman realm—Morocco to the west and Iran to the east—with only minor variations in timing and scope.

4. "Klondike on the Nile" was the telling title David S. Landes chose for chapter 4 in his book to describe the rush of European businessmen and bankers to exploit Egypt in the mid–nineteenth century. See his *Bankers and Pashas: International Finance and Economic Imperialism in Egypt.* Cambridge, MA: Harvard University Press, 1969.

5. Bin Diyaf translation 84–87. References to Bin Diyaf's *Muqaddima* will cite the page(s) of the English translation that follows. Other references from Bin Diyaf's history will list the volume and page(s) of the published Arabic text.

6. The ʿulama' insisted that their position as Shariʿa judges was "not appropriate to engaging in politics." Bin Diyaf Book 4: 248.

7. Sadiqi College (actually equivalent to a secondary school) survived into the Protectorate period and became the principal modernizing influence for generations, playing a role rather like the Syrian Protestant College (later American University of Beirut) in Lebanon or Gordon Memorial College (later Khartoum University) in Sudan. Habib Bourguiba and eight of the eleven members of the first Tunisian cabinet after independence were graduates of Sadiqi College. For an in–depth study of this important educational institution see Noureddine Sraïeb, *Le Collège Sadiki de Tunis: 1875–1956: Enseignement et Nationalisme.* Paris: CNRS, 1995.

8. Rosenthal translation *The Muqaddimah* Volume 1:6.

9. See Bin Diyaf translation, 64-65.

10. See above, pages 11–12.

11. Here Bin Diyaf is following a line from Ibn Khaldun, "The Persians and other nations have such norms." He later cites extensively from Ibn Khaldun's text where this line appears. See Bin Diyaf translation 75 and 91.

12. Bin Diyaf translation 116.

13. Moncef Chenoufi has discovered an English translation published in Athens in 1874 entitled *Necessary Reforms of the Musulman States: Essay*

which forms the first part of the Political and Statistical World entitled The Surest Way to know the State of Nations, but since it does not figure in contemporary or even later sources it must have had little circulation.

14. Ahmed Abdesselem, *Les Historiens Tunisiens des XVIIe, XVIIIe et XIX Siécles: Essai d'historie culturelle.* Paris and Tunis: Librairie C. Klincksieck, 1973.

15. Abdesselem, 287. Also, Bin Diyaf biographies on Muhammad Bayram I (Book 7:30–34), Muhammad Bayram II (Book 7: 158–162), Muhammad Bayram III (Book 8:54–55) and Muhammad Bayram IV (Book 8: 124–126) as well as Larry Barrie, *A Family Odyssey: the Bayrams of Tunis, 1756–1861,* Ph.D. Dissertation, Boston University, 1987 (University Microfilms).

16. Edited by ʿAli ibn al-Tahir al-Shanufi and Riyad al-Marzuqi, volume 2, Tunis, 1999. This entire volume is devoted to Tunisia, the other sections offer encyclopedic coverage of the country with copious annotation by the editors. The notes on the history portion alone fill ninety-six pages.

17. *The Surest Path*, pp. 72–73, 42–43 and 125–28.

18. Of the total 107 pages in the English translation of *The Surest Path,* 56 pages deal directly with Europe, such as pp. 93–96, 99–111, and 137–178.

19. Victor Duruy, *Histoire du moyen âge depuis la chute de l'empire d'occident jusqu'au milieu du Xve siècle.* Paris, Hachette, many editions, and L.A. Sedillot, *Histoire des Arabes.* Paris, 1854.

20. The first sentence of Khayr al-Din's translation from Duruy gives the flavor: "While the people of Europe were lost in the deepest darkness of ignorance, seeing only the slightest light as if through the eye of a needle, there radiated from the Islamic ʿumma' a powerful light of literature, philosophy, the arts, industries, etc. ..." *The Surest Path*, p. 99, where reference to Victor Duruy's influence in Ottoman education reform during the 1860s is given as well.

21. Several of Bin Diyaf's apparent or clear borrowings from *The Surest Path* are cited in the notes to the translation.

22. See Bernard Lewis, *What Went Wrong? Western Impact and Middle Eastern Response.* Oxford: Oxford University Press, 2002, especially pp. 158ff.

23. *The Surest Path*, pp. 80–81.

24. Oxford: Oxford University Press, 1962, especially pp. 81 and 103.

25. Quite inaccurate, he was a Circassian mamluk.

26. See my chapter "Stage Two: The Young Tunisians, or, The Age of Reason" in Charles A. Micaud, et. al., *Tunisia: The Politics of Modernization.* Westport, CN: Praeger, 1964, pp. 22–37 and Charles–Andre Julien, "Colons Francais et Jeunes–Tunisiens, 1882–1912" in *Revue Française d'Histoire d'Outre–Mer* Tome 54 (1967) pp. 87–150.

27. It is not quite clear when or how the usage *qanun* for constitution gave way to *destour,* but Khalifa Chater notes that the Tunisian poet and leading member of the reformist group, Mahmud Qabadu, used both *qanun* and *des-*

tour to describe the Tunisian constitution. See his "Le Constitutionalisme en Tunisie au 19e siècle" *Revue Tunisienne de Sciences Sociales* (1975) p. 244.

CHAPTER ONE: INVOCATION AND INTRODUCTION

1. Both *shari͏̈a* and *shar͏ᶜ* are translated "Religious Law."

2. ᶜAbd al-Rahman Ibn Khaldun (later given the sobriquet *Wali al-Din* [Guardian of the Religion]) was born in Tunis (732/1332) and died at the age of seventy-four in Cairo (808/1406). His active scholarly and political life ranged over the Maghrib, Spain, and, for the last twenty-four years of his life, Egypt. His famous *Muqaddima* (Introduction or Prolegomena) has been aptly characterized as "An Arab Philosophy of History" (the title given to the selections translated and arranged by Charles Issawi—an excellent short study) and he has been compared to the likes of Machiavelli, Bodin, and Vico in his capacity to relate the actual workings of politics. Bin Diyaf, as will become evident, cites Ibn Khaldun often, clearly seeing him as a compelling authority.

3. Died 932/1525–26, author of *Tarikh al-Dawlatayn al-Muwahhidiyya wa al-Hafsiyya* (History of the Almohad and Hafisd Dynasties).

4. Seventeenth century Tunisian historian whose death date is unknown but after 1092/1681–82, the last entry date in his history, *al-Mu'nis fi Akhbar Ifriqiyya wa Tunis* (History of Ifriqiyya and Tunis). See for Ibn Abi Dinar and the next three cited (al-Wazir al-Sarraj, Hammuda ibn ᶜAbd al-ᶜAziz and al-Baji al-Masᶜudi), the excellent study by Ahmed Abdesselem, *Les Historiens Tunisiens des XVIIe, XVIIIe et XIXe Siècles*. Abdesselem lists a French translation of *Al-Mu'nis* by E. Pellissier and C. de Remusat, *Histoire de l'Afrique et de Tunis*. Paris: *Imprimerie Royale*, 1845, but adds that is unreliable.

5. Author (died circa 1149/1736–37) of *al-Hulal al–Sundusiyya fi Al-Akhbar al Tunisiyya*, a general chronicle most interesting for its last chapter, treating the reign of his contemporary and the eponym of the Husaynid dynasty, Husayn ibn ᶜAli (ruled 1705–35).

6. Author (died 1202/1775) of *Kitab al–Bashi* (The Book of the Pasha), scholar and confidant of ᶜAli Pasha (ruled 1735–56), who was the principal subject of his book.

7. Al-Baji al-Masᵓudi (born 1225/1810–11, died 1297/1880) was a contemporary of Bin Diyaf. Treating Tunisia from the advent of Islam, his book is a sparse working, providing, for example, only some thirty pages on the Husaynid period. Abdeselem, *Historiens Tunisiens*, p. 310.

8. This is the part translated here.

CHAPTER TWO: ON GOVERNANCE AND ITS VARIETIES

1. In Islamic law a communal obligation (*fard kifaya*) is one that is satisfied if carried out by a selected number of individuals acting for the community. An individual obligation (*fard ᶜayn*) is incumbent on all Muslims.

2. *Ahl al–hall wa a– ʿAqd*. This designates those empowered to decide, but the concept of who is numbered among those authorized to loosen and bind is never spelled out in Islamic law or political thought. This image of loosening and binding to depict power or authority should strike a familiar chord to Jews and Christians. See Job 38:31 and Matthew 16:19 and 18:18.

3. Al-Asamm (the Deaf), Abu al-ʿAbbas Muhammad ibn Yaʿqub al-Nisaburi (born 247/861, died 346/957–58), a Shafiʿi scholar.

4. For all of Bin Diyaf's many citations from Ibn Khaldun, a reference to Franz Rosenthal's three volume translation of the entire work (Ibn Khaldun, *The Muqaddimah: An Introduction to History* 3 vols. Bollinger Series XLIII. Princeton, NJ: Princeton University Press, 2nd edition, 1967) is given. This first citation is found in Volume 1:390–91.

CHAPTER THREE: ABSOLUTE RULE

1. Shaykh Abu Abdullah Muhammad ibn Yusuf ibn Abu al-Qasim al-ʿAbdiri (died 897/1492), known as al-Mawwaq, was qadi of Granada. His *Sunnan al-Muhtadin fi Maqamat al-Din* (Traditions of the Rightly Guided concerning the Stages of Religion) is a general Maliki treatise on *Shariʿa* conduct and practice.

2. Muhammad ibn al-Walid Tartushi (born 451/1059, died 520/1126).

3. Ibn ʿAbd al-Barr Yusuf ibn Abdullah al-Qartabi (died 463/1070–71).

4. Al-ʿIyad ibn Musa al-Sibti (died 544/1149–50).

5. The collection of *hadiths* assembled by Muslim ibn al-Hajjaj (born 206/821, died 261/875) is deemed one of the six "sound" (*sahih*) collections and is the collection most respected among Maghribi scholars.

6. Ibn al Munasif Muhamad ʿIsa al-Azdi al-Qartabi (died 620/1223–24).

7. Ibn al–Mundhir Muhammad Ibrahim al-Nishapuri, (died 319/931–932).

8. The reformist *Hatt-ı Şerif* [of] *Gulhane* (*Khatt al-Sharif* in Arabic) issued by Ottoman Sultan ʿAbd al-Majid in 1839 looms large, as will be seen, in Bin Diyaf's Introduction. It will be translated consistently as "Noble Rescript."

9. Islamic law divides individual acts into a five part classification: obligatory (*wajib*), recommended (*mandub*), permissible or morally neutral (*mubah*), reprehensible (*makruh*), and forbidden (*haram*).

10. ʿAbd al-Rahman ibn ʿAbd al-Qadir Abu Zayd al-Fasi (died 1096/1684–85).

11. This last sentence does not follow logically from the above seemingly categorical statements about fighting the Kharijites and siding with a ruler, even if unjust. It can perhaps best be interpreted as a cautious hedge, giving the appearance of always lining up (but perhaps only passively?) with the just.

12. Al-Harith Abu ʿAmr (died 250/864–65).

13. ʿUmar ibn ʿAbd al-ʿAziz, the eighth caliph in the Umayyad line, ruled

from 717 to 720. Often cited in the early Islamic sources for his piety and probity, his standing as a model worthy of admiration and emulation approaches that of the first four caliphs—Abu Bakr, ʿUmar ibn al-Khattab, ʿUthman, and ʿAli—the "four rightly guided caliphs."

14. Ibn Hajar al-Asqaani (born 773/1372, died 852/1449), Egyptian *hadith* scholar, judge, and historian.

15. A reference to the first part of the Qur'anic verse 4:59 reading, "O you who believe, obey God and obey the messenger [Muhammad] and those in authority among you." The passage cited below, "And if you have a dispute concerning any matter, refer it to God and to the Messenger," immediately follows.

16. Husayn ibn Muhammad al-Tibi (died 743/1342–43).

17. Mufti and imam of the Zitouna mosque (died 1234/1819). See his biography in Bin Diyaf, Volume 7, no. 72.

18. Muhammad ibn Ahmad al-Fasi (died 1072/1661–62), known as al-Mayyara, author of *Sharh al-Shaykh Mayyara li-Lamiyya al-Zaqqaq* (The Commentary of Shaykh Mayyara on al-Zaqqaq's *Lamiyya*).

19. ʿAli ibn Qasim al-Tijani al-Zaqqaq, a jurist from Fez (died 912/1506–07). The *Manzuma al-Lamiyya* was a textbook on judicial procedures in the form of a long poem (for judges to memorize).

20. Ibn ʿAbd al-Barr (see note 3), author of *Al-Istidhkar li-Madhahib-Fuqaha al-Amsar wa ʿulama' al-Aqtar fi ma Tadammanahu al-Muwatta min maʿani al-Ray wa al-Athar* (Setting out the Legal schools of the Jurisconsults of the cities and the ulama of the countries concerning the meanings of opinions and precedents contained in the *Muwatta*).

21. By ʿAbd al-Rahman ibn ʿAli, ibn al-Daybaʿ (died 944/1537–38), an abridgement of *Jamiʿ al-Usul* by Ibn al-Athir.

22. By Ibn ʿAbd Rabbihi al-Andalusi (860–940).

23. Ahmad ibn Idris al-Qarafi (died 684/1285), wrote *al-Dhakhira* (a six–volume work on Maliki law).

24. Abu Bakr Muhammad ibn ʿAbd Allah, known as Ibn ʿArabi (died 543/1148–49), author of *al-Qabas fi Sharh Muwatta Malik* (A Short Commentary of the *Muwatta* of Malik).

25. Sulayman's constitution (*qanun*) is discussed on pp. 79–81.

26. ʿAbd Allah ibn al-ʿAbbas, born three years before the Hijra and died 68/687–88, usually referred to as Ibn ʿAbbas.

27. Abu al-Walid Ibn Rushd (1058–1126) wrote *Kitab Muqaddamat al-Mumahhadat li-Bayan ma Aqtadathu Rusam al Mudawwanah min al-Ahkam al-Sharʿiyyat wa al-Tahsilat alMahkamat al-Sharʿiyyat li-Ummahat Masa'iliha al-Mushkilat*. This Ibn Rushd was the grandfather of the philosopher Ibn Rushd, known in the West as Averroes.

28. Rosenthal translation Volume 2:103ff.

29. Rosenthal translation Volume 2:55.

30. "Passes away as scum" adopts the phrase found in Qur'an 13:17, which reads in its entirety: "He sends down water from the sky, so that valleys flow according to their measure, and the flood bears on its surface swelling foam like that which they smelt in the fire in order to make ornaments and tools. Thus, God compares the true and the false. As for the foam, it passes away as scum upon the banks, while, as for that which is of use to mankind, it remains in the earth. Thus, God sets forth parables."

31. ʿAbd Allah ibn ʿAli al-Gharnati Ibn al-Azraq (died 896/1490–91).

32. *Wuzara' tanfidh* as opposed to *wuzara' tafwid* (ministers with delegated authority). This two-part classification of ministers, going back to al–Mawardi in his *al-Ahkam al-Sultaniyyah*, is followed by many later writers, including Ibn Khaldun (See Volume 2:10–11 in the Rosenthal translation).

33. *Makhzan* (literally, storehouse) is a common North African term for government. Thus, the Moroccan binary usage *blad al-makhzan* versus *blad al-siba* (land of dissidence), designating the land controlled by the sultan and his forces as opposed to those Moroccan lands beyond his control.

34. Rosenthal translation Volume 2:93, 95.

35. ʿUmar, the second caliph (ruled from 13/634 to 23/644) was assassinated, and while on his deathbed is reported to have chosen a group of leaders (the *shura* or consultation) to select the next caliph.

36. Ahmad ibn ʿAli Maqrizi (1364–1442), author of *Mawaʿiz wa al-Iʿtibar bi Dhikr al-Khitat wa al-Athar* (Exhortations and Considerations in Citing Lands and Traditions).

37. The Barmakid family, father Yahya and his two sons, Jaʿfar and Fadl, held high positions during the caliphate of Harun al-Rashid (786–809) until in 803 Harun had Jaʿfar executed and Yahya and Fadl banished. Historians still speculate over the reason for this sudden, violent reversal of Barmakid fortunes, and the incident stands out as the classic example of the vulnerability of high officials in despotic regimes.

38. Mulay Sulayman ibn Muhammad reigned as sultan of Morocco from 1792 to 1822. It is significant that Bin Diyaf singles him out for praise. Although he was not all that successful in achieving better central government control and public order, Mulay Sulayman was a devout and scholarly ruler of *salafi* orientation. He rejected *bidʿa* (blameworthy innovation) and sought to return the Muslim community to the ideal seen to have been realized in the time of the Prophet and his early followers. In his reservations about what he saw as excesses of saint-worship and the sufi orders, Mulay Sulayman was even inclined to favor the Wahhabis, who in his time had captured the holy cities of Mecca and Madina. See Mohamed El Mansour, *Morocco in the Reign of Mawlay Sulayman*. Cambridgeshire, England: Middle Eastern & North African Studies Press, 1990, especially chapter 4 "Mawlay Sulayman and Religious Reform at the Beginning of the Nineteenth Century," pp. 132–49.

39. Abu ʿAbd Allah Zarruq (died 1238/1822).

40. Abu Ishaq Ibrahim ibn ʿAbd al-Qadir al-Riyahi (died 1266/1850), author of numerous works and the mufti of Tunis in his time. See Bin Diyaf's long and laudatory biographical entry, Volume 7:73–82.

41. Hamuda ruled from 1777 to 1813.

42. Ibn Khaldun argues that states, like individuals, must age and then die. Tyranny, in this view, is not so much the cause as the result of decline. In fact, Ibn Khaldun makes no reference in the passage cited to tyranny or, for that matter, the just ruler. See Ibn Khaldun, *Muqaddima*, Rosenthal translation Volume 1:336–46. Bin Diyaf's following paragraph may be seen as an effort to move beyond Ibn Khaldun's deterministic interpretation.

CHAPTER FOUR: REPUBLICAN RULE

1. The branches of *fiqh* (*furuʿ al-fiqh*) are the specific norms or the literature setting out the rules of *Shariʿa* (Religious Law). The roots (*usul al-fiqh*) treat the sources and methodology guiding the understanding of Revelation. And *fiqh*, itself, is the discipline describing and explaining the *Shariʿa*.

2. Ibrahim ibn Ibrahim ibn al-Hasan al-Laqani, Maliki jurist (died 1041/1631) whose summary of Maliki doctrines in dogmatics and law (*Jawharat al-Tawhid* or The Essence of Unity) has been a popular reference work among Maliki scholars.

3. The people of Mecca did offer allegiance to the second Hafsid ruler, Mustansir I ibn Yahya in 657/1258–59. Mustansir, who had come to power in 647/1249 (died 675/1276–77) later confronted the forces of the Eighth Crusade against Tunis led by French King Louis IX (1214–1270, reigned 1226–70) that landed in Tunis in July 1270. When sickness swept over the Crusader camp, killing even Louis IX, this campaign was ignominiously withdrawn.

4. *Sahib al Qanun*, or more often in Ottoman sources, *al-qanuni*, known in the West at Sulayman the Magnificent.

5. *Al-Din al-Muhammadi*. It is often, and rightly, pointed out that Muslims dislike being called "Muhammadan" since that suggests Muhammad is to Islam as Christ is to Christianity. The Qur'an and Islamic doctrine make it crystal clear that Muhammad was only a man. Muslims, accordingly, would classify the Christian concept of the incarnation as *shirk* (associating any person or thing with God), among the worst of sins in Islam. Even so, one does come across Muslim references to "the Muhammadan religion" or similar constructions using the Prophet Muhammad's name in this fashion.

6. The second part of the Introduction, volume one of Bin Diyaf's eight-volume history, traces summarily the history of Tunisia during the Islamic period from the arrival of the Muslim Arabs in the mid-seventh century until the sixteenth century with the exploits of Khayr al-Din Barbarossa and the Ottoman conquest.

7. Muslim writers use both Constantinople (*Kustantiniyya*) and Istanbul to refer to the Ottoman capital, the latter being more common. Another interesting touch, Istanbul is often written in Arabic to read "Islambul."

CHAPTER FIVE: GOVERNMENT LIMITED BY LAW (*QANUN*)

1. A paraphrase of the *hadith* "the believers stand by their commitments."

2. Mustawrid ibn Shaddaad, a Qurayshi companion of the Prophet, died 45/665–666 in Alexandria.

3. This appears also in Khayr al-Din, *The Surest Path* Arabic pp. 20–21, English translation p. 96.

4. The story in slightly different form is in Khayr al-Din, *The Surest Path*, Arabic p. 17, English translation p. 93.

5. This is a translation of *Evening Entertainment or Delineations of the Manners and Customs of Various Nations interspersed with geographical notices, historical and biographical anecdotes, and descriptions in natural history designed for the instruction and amusement of youth* by G. B. Depping (1784–1853) published in 1812. The Bulaq Press in Cairo (set up by Muhammad Ali to translate Western works) produced an Arabic translation in 1833.

6. Muhammad ibn Musa Damiri (1341?–1405) author of *Hayat al Hayawan al Kubra* (The Greater Book on Large Animals).

7. *Hizbullah* (Party of God) is the Qur'anic label adopted by several modern Islamist groups. The expression "Party of God" appears also in Qur'an 5:56.

8. Using the two words *munkar* and *ma`ruf*, Bin Diyaf is clearly referring to the *hisba* charge to "command the good and forbid the evil" (*al-ʿamr bi al-ma`ruf wa al-nahiya ʿan al-munkar*).

9. Written by Mehmed Es`ad, it was also translated into French by A.P. Caussin de Perceval, *Precis historique de la destruction du corps des janissaires par le sultan Mahmoud, en 1826*. Paris, 1833.

10. Nizami stems from the term in Ottoman Turkish *Nizam-i Cedid* (New Order, Arabic *Nizam al-Jadid*) to indicate the westernized military corps created by Ottoman Sultan Selim III in 1793. The 1807 Janissary revolt forced him to disband this new corps, and soon thereafter came his abdication and execution. After Sultan Mahmud II secured his position, he reinstituted the idea of Nizami forces and succeeded where Selim III had failed by putting down yet another Janissary revolt in 1826. Nizami came be adopted to describe all such westernizing innovations, and the covering title for the great age of such Ottoman reforms (1839–76) in all fields—*Tanzimat*—is from the same Arabic n–z–m root.

11. The translation of the Turkish original by Halil Inalcik, to be found in J. C. Hurewitz (ed.), *The Middle East and North Africa in World Politics: A*

Documentary Record. New Haven, CN: Yale University Press, 1975, Volume 1, No. 89:269–71, stops at this point.

12. The Prophet Muhammad's cloak is believed to have been in the possession of the Abbassid caliphs and then taken from the last of the Abbassid line by Sultan Selim I when the Ottomans captured Egypt. Thereafter, it served as the Ottoman royal standard.

13. Fuʿad Pasha (1815–1869), five times Ottoman foreign minister and twice grand vizier, was one of the three leaders during the era of the *Tanzimat* reforms, along with ʿAli Pasha (1815–1871) and their mentor, Rashid Pasha (1800–1858).

14. *Siyasa Shar`iyya*, Fauzi M. Najjar suggests, might best be defined as "government in accordance with the revealed law." See p. 96 of his "Siyasa in Islamic Political Philosophy" in *Islamic Theology and Philosophy: Studies in Honor of George F. Hourani*, ed. Michael M. Marmura. Albany: State University of New York Press, 1984, pp. 92–110 and 295–97. Much more, however, can said about these two words that would seem to link politics or statecraft with religion or Religious Law. It is perhaps significant that Bin Diyaf does not assume his readers can take the measure of the term. He immediately follows his use of *Siyasa Shar*ᶜ*iyya* with a general explanation of its meaning. On this subject see, in addition to Najjar, Bernard Lewis, "Siyasa" in *In Quest of an Islamic Humanism: Arabic and Islamic Studies in Memory of Mohamed al-Nowaihi*, ed. A. H. Green. Cairo, The American University in Cairo Press, 1984, pp. 3–14 and Ahmed Abdesselem, *Dirasat fi Mustalih al-Siyasiyya ᶜand al-ᶜArab*. Tunis: *Studies on Arab Political Vocabulary*, 1978, pp. 9–39.

15. Ibn al-Azraq. See chapter 3, note 31.

16. Tahtawi (1801–1873) spent the years from 1826 to 1831 in Paris as imam of the student mission sent to France by Muhammad ᶜAli. An excellent short account of his activities and influence is found in Albert Hourani's *Arabic Thought in the Liberal Age*, pp. 68–87.

17. Rosenthal translation Volume 1:385–86.

18. Ibrahim ibn Musa Shatibi (died 1388).

19. In Muslim law, those living in a land that comes under Muslim rule will not be obliged to embrace Islam if they are *ahl al-kitab* (people of the book, that is, Jews or Christians). All others, in theory, are to be killed or enslaved, but actual practice extended to include others as well. Non-Muslims living under Muslim rule are designated *ahl al-dhimma* (people of the covenant) and the individual having this status a *dhimmi*. The *dhimmi* obtains protection and has a number of rights, but also disabilities by comparison to the Muslim. He must, for example, pay a special tax (*jizya*). To label the *dhimmi* a second-class citizen is anachronistic. Defining rights and duties in a political community according to religious affiliation was the norm in premodern times, both in Christendom and Islam. The radically different notion of a common and equal citizenship, indeed of a patriotism, shared by all living in a specific political community was becoming increasingly the norm in Europe (but to avoid

lapsing into another example of anachronistic thinking one should recall the limits on the rights of atheists and Jews in the writings of John Locke, the late date [1829] of the Catholic Emancipation Act and the even later date [1867] when Lionel de Rothschild was permitted to take his seat in Parliament without being required to take a Christian oath of office). Bin Diyaf offers here what might be dubbed an especially benign interpretation of the classical *dhimma*. He does not directly address the intrusive new concept of equality of citizenship.

20. ⁽Ali ibn Ahmad ibn Hazm (994–1064), wrote *Maratib al-Ijma` fi al-*⁽*Ibadat wa al-Mu*⁽*amalat wa al-I`tiqadat* (Areas of Consensus on Rituals, Transactions, and Beliefs).

21. Shihab al-Din Abu al-⁽Abbas Ahmad ibn Idris ibn ⁽Abd al-Rahmanm al-Sanhaji, known as al- Qarafi (died 684/1285), an Egyptian Maliki scholar, author of *Al-Furuq* ("Different [legal cases]") and many other works.

22. *Al-Ashbah wa al-Naza*⁽*ir* ⁽*ala Madhhab Abu Hanifa* (Analogues and Comparabilities in the Legal School of Abu Hanifa) by Zayn al–Din ibn Ibrahim ibn Nujaym al–Misri (died 1563).

23. Al-Mawardi (974–1058), perhaps the most influential Muslim thinker on the theory of the caliphate. See H. A. R. Gibb, "Al-Mawardi's Theory of the Caliphate" in his *Studies on the Civilization of Islam*, Stanford J. Shaw and William L. Polk, eds. Boston: Beacon Press, 1962, and chapter 4 "Al-Mawardi: Wizara and Imara" of *State and Government in Medieval Islam* by Ann K.S. Lambton, Oxford: Oxford University Press, 1981.

24. This story is told quite differently in *The Surest Path*, Arabic pp. 38–39, English p. 121.

25. Literally, the men of consultation—*rijal al-shura*.

26. The duty of *hisba* embraces the broad Islamic injunction to command the right and forbid the wrong (*al-*⁽*amr fi al-ma*⁽*ruf wa al-nahiya* ⁽*an al-munkar*), a binary trope often occurring the Qur'an, for example 3:104, 110, and 114; 7:157; 9:71 and 112; and 22:41). The *hisba* office is that of the individual charged with enforcing these duties.

27. Seemingly, there is a difference between *Shari*⁽*a* and *Shar*⁽*i* court according to the nature of the cases presented.

28. No source cited.

29. Hammuda ibn ⁽Abd al ⁽Aziz (died 1202/1775) author of *Kitab al–*Bashi. See notes 4 and 6.

30. The *mukhazaniyya* were either the tribal cavalry forces who participated as irregulars in tax collecting expeditions (*mahalla*) and other security duties or, more broadly, those in political or military positions of government—roughly "men of the sword" as opposed to "men of the pen."

31. *Zabaniyya*, "angels of wrath," appears once in the Qur'an (96:18).

32. A variant reading in another manuscript is "I have expatiated in this

matter of kingship, but perhaps the state of the discipline of history makes that necessary. Some who are associated with the sciences do not approve of it. They see it as a blameworthy innovation (*bidᶜa*) since it is to copy the ways of non-Muslims, plus other such notions that it would pain me to relate."

CHAPTER SIX: CONCLUSION

1. From a *hadith*, not a Qur'anic citation.

2. Muhammad ibn Hamida ibn al–Khuja (died 1279/1862), Tunisian Hanafi scholar. See Bin Diyaf's biography, Volume 8:127–29.

3. Taken from Qur'an 9:40, which lauds Abu Bakr's faithfulness to the Prophet Muhammad and his mission.

4. Literally, "the concluding musk," a standard expression taken from Qur'an 83:25–26: Those accepted into paradise "will be given to drink of a pure beverage, sealed, whose seal is musk—let all those who aspire aspire for this."

CHAPTER SEVEN: THE 1857 FUNDAMENTAL PACT (ᶜAHD AL-AMAN)

1. This refers, in rhymed prose (*sajʾ*) to the canonical five-part breakdown of all human acts ranging from forbidden to obligatory. See page 140, note nine.

2. This, Turkish for province, is the word most often used to describe Tunisia in the *ᶜAhd*. *Mamlaka* (kingdom), interestingly, which suggests sovereignty, is avoided in the text, but then is used in the closing sentence. *Dawla* (now the Arabic word for state but still at this time meaning dynasty) is used once.

Selected Bibliography

Abdesselem, Ahmed. *Dirasat fi Mustali' al-Siyasiyya 'and al-'Arab* [Studies on Arab Political Vocabulary]. Tunis: Société Tunisienne de Diffusion, 1978, 167 pages. This title is misleading in its apparent breadth. This is very much a study of Tunisia, concentrating on the nineteenth century. In three compact chapters Abdesselem examines how first Ibn Khaldun and then Khayr al-Din al-Tunisi and Bin Diyaf used the following terms in their *Muqaddima-s*: *siyasa* (politics), *mulk* (kingship), *dawla* (state), *wazi*[c] (restrainer), [c]*asabiyya* (group solidarity), *shura* (consultation), and *ahl al-hall wa al-'aqd* (those of loosening and binding).

———. *Ibn Abi Diyaf: Hayatuhu wa Manzilatuhu wa Muntakhabat min* [c]*Atharihi* [Ibn Abi Diyaf: His Life and His Standing with Selections from his Works]. Tunis: Al-Dar al-[c]Arabiyya lil Kitab, 1984, 125 pages. A fine short study of Bin Diyaf, his life, work, and influence in no more than thirty pages followed by selections from his writings, mainly from the *Ithaf* but also Bin Diyaf's fascinating response to a series of questions posed by European intellectuals concerning the status of women in Tunisia.

———. *Les Historiens Tunisiens des XVIIe, XVIIIe et XIXe Siècles: Essai d'histoire culturelle*. Paris and Tunis: Librairie C. Klincksieck, 1973, 590 pages. A masterful study of Tunisian historiography during the three decades covered. Relevant for the study of Bin Diyaf and his times are chapter 3 "Le Milieu culturel de 1830 à 1890" and the specific studies of Khayr al-Din (pp. 325–31) and Bin Diyaf (pp. 332–82). Bin Diyaf also figures prominently in his "Livre Troiseme: Conceptions, Méthodes et Procédés des Historiens."

Berchet, Leon. "En marge du Pacte fundamental," *Revue tunisienne* New Series, No. 37, lst trimester, 1939, pp. 67–86. A French translation of a brief Bin Diyaf wrote arguing that Jewish subjects should be permitted to serve as members of the Grand Council provided for in the Tunisian Constitution with the response by Gen. Hussein (a close colleague of Khayr al-Din and generally deemed one of the reformers) rejecting Bin Diyaf's argument.

———. *Dustur: Survey of the Constitutions of the Arab and Muslim States* (reprinted with additional material from the second edition of the *Encyclopedia of Islam*). Leiden, Netherlands: E. J. Brill, 1966. Twenty different country studies leading off, quite rightly, with Tunisia. A good statement, but all too brief, pp. 1–5.

Bdira, Mezri. *Relations internationals et sous–développement: La Tunisie 1857–1864*. Stockholm, Sweden: Acta Universitatis Upsaliensis, 1978, 194 pages. An especially well-organized and perceptive study that has the advantage of concentrating on just those years in Tunisia most important

149

to the subject treated here. Based on a thorough use of the Tunisian governmental archives and also appropriate Ottoman archives.

Chater, Khalifa. "'Awda ila al-Ithaf " [Returning to the Ithaf] in volume one of the 1999 edition of the Ithaf published by the Tunisian Ministry of Culture. A good, short (eighteen-page) summation of Bin Diyaf's life and times and appraisal of his work. Chater also recounts the publishing history of the Ithaf and notes his other writings.

————. "Le constitutionalisme en Tunisie au 19eme siècle," Revue tunisienne des Sciences Sociales No. 40–43, 1975, pp. 243–272. Chater offers a nuanced account of Tunisia's constitutional period, enriched by his use of documentation from the Tunisian National Archives, especially for the period 1861–64. He emphasizes that the general Tunisian awareness— both by the government and the people—of the extent to which the ʿAhd al-Aman and the constitution were largely imposed by Europe was a major factor in fostering antipathy to this brief constitutional regime. He sees the constitutional institutions of representation as having become little more than a façade papering over continued absolutism. Chater also draws out Bin Diyaf's own reservations about the "people" as agitation moved toward a revolutionary situation.

Demeerseman, R. P. André. "Formulations de l'idée de patrie en Tunisie (1837–1872)." Institut des belles lettres Arabes. 113 1eme trimester, 1966, pp. 35–71 and 114–15 2eme trimester, 1966 pp. 109–42. A discussion, relying largely on Bin Diyaf's Ithaf, of the evolving usages of political terms such as dawla, mamlaka, and watan. Some overlap with but also a useful complement to Abdesselem's Dirasat, cited above.

Ganiage, Jean. Les origins du protectorat français en Tunisie: 1861–1881. Paris: Presses Universitaires de France, 1959, 776 pages. A huge book, the fruit of a French doctorat d'état. The bibliography alone is a full fifty-five pages. This is truly in-depth diplomatic history, giving not just the details of consuls, cabinets and commissions but a thorough presentation of the Tunisian state and society during those years, the 1864 revolt, and much more. I have earlier cited this as an absolutely essential source for nineteenth-century Tunisian history (in my The Tunisia of Ahmad Bey, 1837–1855, pp. 389–90) but added that it was "faulted by a consistently sardonic attitude, a poor grasp of Muslim institutions, and an inability or unwillingness to appreciate the bewildering cross-currents faced by the early generations of Muslim political Westernizers." I would now, years later, want to tone down, but not repudiate, that criticism.

Jdey, Ahmed. Ahmed ibn Abi Dhiaf, Son Oeuvre et sa pensée: Essai d'Histoire culturelle. Zaghouan, Tunisia: Fondation Temimi pour le Recherche Scientifique et l'Information (FTERSI), 1996, 528 pages. Another large doctoral dissertation later published in Tunisia. Loosely organized and long-winded, it can nevertheless serve as a useful reference. Examples of his wide-ranging coverage: a full eighty pages summarizing the different critiques of Bin Diyaf by his contemporaries and later scholars, both

Tunisian and foreign, eight pages proposing an alternative translation of *Ithaf Ahl al-Zaman* to that given by Abdesselem, and separate chapters on the roles of Ibn Khaldun, Khayr al-Din al-Tunisi, and al-Tahtawi in Bin Diyaf's *Ithaf*.

Majallat al-Ithaf. *Multaqa Ibn Abi Dinar lil Fikr al-Siyasi wa al-Ijtima'i al-Hadith* [Rendezvous of Ibn Abi Diyaf with Modern Political and Social Thought]. Tunis: Matba° al-Munazzimat al°Arabiyya lil Tarbiyya wa al-Thaqafa wa al-°Ulum, 1989, 164 pages. Articles by fourteen different Tunisian scholars that appeared in the journal *Ithaf* in 1979, 1980, and 1983. Short and necessarily overviews, they do not add to the information or analysis given in the works of Abdesselem and Tlili, but they do reveal the broad scholarly interest in Bin Diyaf and his *Ithaf* among contemporary Tunisian scholars. They also indicate the diverse range of interpretations concerning him and his work. Noteworthy are the articles by Ahmad Tuwayli and Jum°a Shaykha, pp. 81–107.

al-Nayfur, Mustafa. "Hawla Tawbat al-Mustabid" (*Tajriba Tunisiyya Sabiqa–°Ahd al-Aman–1864)* [Concerning a Despot's Repentance–An Earlier Tunisian Example, °Ahd al-Aman–1864]. *Al-Hiwar* 20/1991, pp. 49–82. Relying largely on Bin Diyaf's *Ithaf*, al-Nayfur uses the history of Tunisia's constitutional period to test his working hypothesis that despotic rulers do not readily repent of their ways and outside pressure on them to do so has been too sporadic to effectively impose change. The despotic ruler knows how to concede only as much as is necessary to counter Western pressures. The West, in turn, will back off from supporting such reforms. He draws parallels with contemporary Western–Third World confrontations on issues of human rights.

Raymond, Andre. "La France, La Grande–Bretagne et le Probléme de la Reforme à Tunis (1855–1857)." *Etudes maghrebines: Mélanges Charles Andre Julien*, Pierre Marthelot and Andre Raymond, eds. Paris: Presse Universitaires de France, 1964, pp. 137–64. Details how the British and French consuls, working together and often going beyond their governments' instructions, obliged the bey to proclaim the °Ahd al-Aman. Interestingly, these consular officials believed that Bin Diyaf was to be numbered among those "fanatics" opposing the °Ahd al-Aman. They saw Khayr al-Din and his father-in-law, Mustafa Khaznadar, as leading those advocating reform.

Tlili, Béchir. *Études d'Histoire Sociale Tunisienne de XIXe Siecle*. Tunis, Université de Tunis, 1974. Tlili gathers in his book ten studies, all relevant to this subject, that had appeared earlier in different journals. Two treat Muhammad Bayram V, two Khayr al-Din al-Tunisi, and two Bin Diyaf: "La Notion d'État dans le pensée et l'oeuvre de A. Ibn Abi Diyaf" and "A l'aube du Mouvement de Réformes a Tunis: Un important document de B. Diyaf sur la feminisme." Two of the other four studies deal with history and historiography: "L'Occident dans la Pensée sociale et politique arabe moderne et contemporaire" and "La Notion d'Umran dans le Pensée Tunisienne pre–Coloniale."

Womble, Theresa Liane. *Early Constitutionalism in Tunisia, 1857–1864: Reform and Revolt*. Ph.d. dissertation, Princeton University, 1997, 265 pages (text 185 pages, appended Arabic texts and official French translations of the ʿAhd al-Aman and the constitution plus annotated bibliography add eighty pages). A well-organized study. Chapter 4, "Constitutional Government in Tunisia," is especially useful in presenting the members of the *Majlis al-Akhbar* and giving details of their proceedings during their short tenure from 1861 to 1864. There is also a concluding chapter setting Tunisia's constitutional experience in comparative perspective.

Index